mjf

Personal Finance

A Practical Guide

MICHAEL TAILLARD

MJF BOOKS
New York

Published by MJF Books
Fine Communications
322 Eighth Avenue
New York, NY 10001

Personal Finance: A Practical Guide
LC Control Number: 2017954421
ISBN 978-1-60671-384-6

This book was previously titled *Introducing Personal Finance: A Practical Guide.*

This edition is published by MJF Books in arrangement with Icon Books Ltd.

Designed by Lisa Chovnick

Printed in the United States of America.

QF 10 9 8 7 6 5 4 3 2 1

To those who work yet struggle.

To those who struggle to work.

To those who invent, or write, or dream
without financing.

To those investors and entrepreneurs
without funding.

You are the unsung heroes of innovation—
the discontented geniuses too often left without
witness.

Find here tools to thrive in a world which
prevents you from achieving your potential
yet punishes lack of success.

CONTENTS

Personal Finance

– 1 –

GETTING STARTED

There are a number of different philosophies on finance, some stating that money is 'the root of all evil' or that money is a valueless fraud, which has tricked the world into pursuing its own demise. Other, less depressing views on finance see money as a medium of exchange, or as value itself. Most people don't even care what the underlying nature of money is, so long as they continue to have enough of it to pay their expenses, but the nature of money is a representation of human nature, the way we coordinate societies. Unless you understand the nature of money and finance, you cannot possibly hope to effectively manage either. So, before explaining how to manage your finances, we must first explain exactly what you will be managing, as well as how to begin.

WHAT IS FINANCE?

Money is debt. Surely it's rare that a person will provide their services to customers or employers for free, but if the recipient of those services has nothing you want in return at the moment, then the exchange becomes more difficult. They could offer you a credit for their own goods or services, but there are times where a barter transaction like this simply will not work, either because one person has nothing the other wants or the timing is wrong. Instead, they give you a credit which you can give to anyone else, which will still be honoured regardless of who has it. This trait is called transferability, and it's what allows money to be given to others in exchange for their services, and after several intervals of exchange; eventually, it will likely be given back to the person who originally gave it to you, by whomever needs his services. Money, then, is nothing more than a form of measurement, providing a numerical way to record the amount of value in goods or services that are owed and can be transferred freely between people, which is exactly how money gets its value.

Transferability: A characteristic (of a credit) of being able to readily transfer or exchange ownership.

Money: Any store of resource value owed to the owner.

Money, by itself, has almost no value at all. Philosopher of the Scottish Enlightenment Adam Smith saw this as the paradox of value, wherein water is crucially useful yet people place so much more value on gold. This seeming paradox is resolved exactly for that reason; however—because water is so useful and is used in such huge quantities—it is difficult to maintain as a unit of measurement, since it has a tendency to be consumed, expire or otherwise become difficult to transport. That's not to say that these types of currencies don't exist, since spices, silks and especially salt have all been used to great success as types of hard currencies by merchants, traders and entire civilizations—even cigarettes are effective as a currency in prisons—but they still hold the same challenges as attempting to use water as a currency. By contrast, gold has almost no intrinsic usefulness, which is exactly why it works well as a way to measure value. The gold itself has little value, but the underlying resources which it represents are those upon which we place value. Since it is rare, light and lasts indefinitely, it is simple to carry small quantities of gold that will be sufficient to partake in even large transactions.

Whether we are talking about gold, silver or copper coins, paper or digital cryptocurrencies, like Bitcoins (or any other transferable unit of value measurement), it is all fiat currency. Fiat currency is any currency whose value is derived from people's willingness to use it. The simple fact that you are willing to provide services to your employer in exchange for a currency is what gives that currency its value. Whether that money has any functional purpose on its own is irrelevant, so long as you can achieve those functional purposes by giving the currency away to others. Nearly every exchange transfers value in two directions: someone provides goods or services of useful value, and in exchange they are given by someone else a measure of value owed to them which they can then exchange for something else of useful value.

Every single exchange establishes not just the money-value of the goods and services, but also the resource value of the money. When you buy something, you have voted and said that you agree the resources you are receiving have value equal to or greater than whatever you did to earn the money, which is the core of finance.

KEY TERM

Fiat currency: Any currency which derives its value from the value of the resource exchanges it represents.

Whereas money is the unit we use to measure a debt of resource value, finance—which studies the way in which money is used—becomes a study of human behaviour. Finance gives us a profound look into the human mind as we come to understand the value people place on specific types of goods and services, on their own time, on the potential to earn more money or on the amount of risk inherent in every financial decision we make. Each time you buy or sell something, two people have voted to agree that the value of the exchange was comparable, with each party earning more value in the exchange than they would have by keeping the resources or money they already owned. By contrast, by refusing to buy or sell at a given price, you have voted to say that the value is not comparable, though others might disagree—even if you do not buy or sell the thing in question at a given price, someone else may be willing to accommodate that price. We can look deep into the priorities and values that an entire society holds by looking at prices, as higher prices indicate that people place greater value on something, while lower prices indicate that people, on average, place lower value on something. All the needs, and desires, and hopes, and dreams, and comforts, and resentments, and jealousies which exist within an entire culture, then, can be understood in terms of price, money, and exchange—such is finance.

When doing anything related to financial management, you are actually managing your values. All the work you have ever done, everything you will ever own, your quality of life, your hopes for the future, your tastes and opinions, and even your personality are all encompassed in your personal finances. Each financial decision you make is an expression of your life and your mind, so much so that a person's financial well-being plays a critical role in their emotional state, as several studies have shown rich people truly are happier and more confident, while those who struggle financially suffer the stress and hardship that comes with uncertainty and loss, and trouble with money is the most commonly reported cause for divorce. Financial management actually has very little to do with money—money is just a unit of measurement—financial management is about taking control of your life.

COLLECTING FINANCIAL INFORMATION

You can't make decisions about your finances until you have some information with which to work; otherwise you are simply guessing. A common beginner's error is to simply keep a written record of all money earned and spent. While this is elegant in its simplicity and seems reasonable if people were completely rational, the truth is that people are not completely rational. Besides being extremely time-consuming and tedious, making people prone to give up, when you pay extra attention to your spending behaviours, those behaviours fundamentally change. In a psychological anomaly known as the 'observation effect', discussed in more detail in chapter 10, when people pay extra close attention to their spending behaviours, they also tend to be more careful with their spending—they will take the extra time to consider how important a purchase really is to them, which fundamentally improves their finances. Since improving your finances starts with understanding what your normal financial behaviour is like, you are going to need to use some other method of getting that information.

Lagging indicators, which is information collected in hindsight, allow you to assess your financial behaviour over some period of time in the recent past. Keeping your receipts has been a very popular method since even before money was commonly used; it is very effective but also very time-consuming, and receipts are easily lost or damaged. With the invention of both credit and debit cards came the bank statement, which can include your transaction history when requested—a list of your earnings and spending with labels reasonably accurate enough to trace the types and locations of transactions. Though debit cards work the same as normal money in most ways, credit cards accrue interest, which means you have to pay back more than you spent. So, if you plan to use credit cards to track your spending, always make sure to pay back the balance before the interest accrual date (another thing people tend to get lazy about, resulting in higher costs than the value of your purchases). Internet banking has been another boon for tracking financial behaviour, since everything you do can be recorded and referenced easily from any location with internet access.

When recording or evaluating your financial records, it's also important to recognize that every transaction is two-way. In a simple example, imagine you are transferring money from your bank account to your investment account—even though the value of your investments has increased as a result, the value of your bank account has decreased. The wages you earn from your work will increase the value of your bank account, but decrease the value of wages still owed to you (sometimes called 'wages receivable'). While this process of financial record keeping, known as 'double-entry accounting', will be explained in more detail in chapter 3, for now just remember that every financial action has an equal and opposite reaction, and that when you are recording or evaluating your records, every change will correspond to a different, opposite change.

KEY TERM **Lagging indicators**: Measurements of past events that allow you to assess financial behaviour over a period of time.

Scheduling

The frequency with which you address individual elements of your finances will vary from person to person, but there are some general guidelines. If you don't revisit your finances frequently enough, then you will miss opportunities and increase waste, but if you revisit them too often, you will become hyperaware of every minor fluctuation, thereby increasing your propensity to erroneously respond to unimportant information and to stress yourself to the brink of madness. For example, unless you are an active day-trader, if you check your stocks every single day, you are likely to perceive patterns or movements which simply don't exist. Our minds are engineered to seek trends and patterns, which is why we see faces in objects like the moon or carpeting. This pattern-seeking behaviour can also cause us to respond to financial information that is completely meaningless to everyone except the most active of securities traders, who now use computer algorithms anyway, making the minute-by-minute stock update a mere re-enactment of now ancient finance.

Each person should be checking their finances as frequently as they need to be responsive. For example, if your income and spending stay very consistent every month, you keep your bills on auto-pay and you have a bit of extra money in the bank in case of emergencies, then you don't need to manage your banking or bills as carefully. By contrast, if you are just barely paying your bills, get paid at the end of each day and have inconsistent spending, then you will need to pay much closer attention. The former person, with steady finances, would likely be safe reviewing their accounts on a monthly or even quarterly basis, while the person with greater financial volatility should probably check their status once or twice per week. If you are managing investment accounts, then how often you revisit your investments depends not only on your investing strategy, but also the type of account you are managing (i.e., brokerage vs. retirement, managed vs. unmanaged, etc.—all discussed throughout several chapters of this book). In order to know how frequently to check each aspect of your financial management, first ask how frequently each aspect is going to deviate from your expectations. This book will help you answer that question.

Integration

The final point to make before we get started with actual financial management is that everything is easier when it's integrated. Financial management uses a lot of data, a lot of calculations and a lot of reports, and they all connect together like pieces of a puzzle. Managing your finances is so much quicker and easier when the data from one report is automatically inserted into all the other reports that rely on that piece of data. In Charles Dickens' *A Christmas Carol*, Bob Cratchit is an old-fashioned bookkeeper, doomed to flip through countless accounts and ledgers to reference and copy the same information over and over—a Sisyphus of the age of merchants and bankers. Now that we have computers, even the simplest spreadsheet or database software can turn weeks' worth of work into a single day's job. Each chapter of this book contains unique information and can be read on its own; however, each contributes useful information to decisions that can be made in every aspect of your finances, such that you will get the most out of your reading by working through the whole book. By automating the overlap using programs from Microsoft Office or Intuit, and programming languages like SAS and SQL, not only does basic financial management become much simpler, but customized financial tools can be developed that push the cutting edge of what's possible and allow your average person to compete with major hedge funds, in their own way.

– 2 –

BUDGETING

People tend to have the wrong idea about what budgeting is supposed to be. For most, a budget is merely a way to keep track of their spending, intended to help them from spending more than they earn, a goal in which they far too frequently fail. This view of budgeting leaves people financially stagnant, simply working to pay their bills, willing to overpay for expensive items through debt simply because they have some extra money for which they have no plans. This fundamentally flawed view of budgeting as a list of expenditures not only causes people to be wasteful with their money, but also to miss vital opportunities with which they can improve their income and optimize the value of their assets.

What most people think of as a budget is actually closer to a simplified form of a personal income statement: a report that tracks income and expenditures.

The goal of creating a quality budget, by contrast, is to manage the allocation of assets—a planning tool used to collect information and make decisions regarding the manner in which you use the resources available to you. Rather than being focused on setting limitations to your expenditures, a well-made budget will provide detailed information about how you distribute your resources and how you can optimize your finances in the future.

Budget: A periodic estimation of resource volume and distribution.

Personal income statement: A report of a person's or household's income, expenditures and financial gains and losses.

PERSONAL INCOME STATEMENT

An income statement is a simple list of the money you make and the money you spend. It's a tool intended to help identify whether you are earning or losing money and the causes of these outcomes, and to track changes in them over time. While many people inappropriately try to use their budget to accomplish these goals, it's actually the income statement which is used to determine how much money you are earning and spending. The income statement is arranged as follows:

Net sales—This is the total amount of income you earn from your primary employment (not including one-time earnings like inheritances or winnings) before you pay taxes, your bills or anything else. If you have multiple sources of income, make sure to distinguish them and list the amount earned from each source, in addition to the sum total from all sources.

COGS—The cost of goods sold (COGS) is a standard consideration on company income statements but all too frequently gets ignored on personal income statements, despite its critical importance. COGS is the total amount you spend in order to earn your income, including the cost of commuting, uniforms or professional clothing, networking and other professional social engagements, and so forth. Any money which you spend exclusively for the purpose of earning your wages should be included. Some people prefer to list this as a single, aggregate cost rather than listing each cost component individually, but it's recommended that you include each component in addition to the total—not only is it more informative in managing your costs, but it's also beneficial when filing your taxes.

Gross margin—The gross margin is calculated easily by starting with your total net sales and then subtracting your total COGS. This is an extremely important value because it tells you what your true take-home pay is for the period. Depending on where you live, this is also likely to be the same value as your taxable income, since many administrations allow tax deductions on business expenses.

Operational expenses—This includes all the other money you spend. Anything you feel you need to spend in order to sustain your daily life is considered an operational expense. Any money you spend on food, clothing not exclusive to work, entertainment, insurance and everything else is included here. Given the potentially broad nature of the types of expenses which can be included here, it's usually prudent to lump similar items together. Rather than listing your beer purchases for the month, for example, you might include it as an 'entertainment' cost.

One-time earnings/losses—This includes any money you earn or spend which is a one-off; in other words, any income or expenses which are not typical for you. This value can be positive or negative, depending on what's happened to you during the period. Costs associated with natural disasters or medical conditions can be included here, as can inheritances and gambling winnings/losses.

EBIT—Your earnings before interest and taxes (EBIT) are easily calculated: start with your gross margin, subtract your total operational expenses and then factor in your one-time earnings or losses (by adding or subtracting, respectively). This is all the money you have which you haven't spent and don't plan to spend in the immediate future.

Taxes and interest—If you pay taxes or interest on debt, then include everything you pay for either of these in the period here. This is an important category on the income statement because it gives you information about the costs associated with funding your earnings and expenses using debt or government services—a concept which will be discussed in greater detail in chapter 5.

Net income—This is the last item on your income statement. Start with your EBIT, then subtract your taxes and interest payments. This is the amount of money that you will put into investments or savings. This value is absolutely critical to watch for trends and to carefully manage because this is the amount by which your total wealth either increases or decreases for the period.

TRY IT NOW!

It seems like a lot to remember, but as long as you keep track of your financial information, the hardest part is just remembering where to include each item. In the end, your income statement should look something like this:

Net Sales Source 1	$XX.xx
Net Sales Source 2	$XX.xx
Total Net Income	$XX.xx
COGS Source 1	$XX.xx
COGS Source 2	$XX.xx
COGS Source 3	$XX.xx
Total COGS	$XX.xx

Gross Margin	$XX.xx
Operational Expense 1	$XX.xx
Operational Expense 2	$XX.xx
Operational Expense 3	$XX.xx
Total Operational Expenses	$XX.xx
One-Time Earnings/Losses	$XX.xx
EBIT	$XX.xx
Tax and Interest Payments	$XX.xx
Net Income	$XX.xx

If you put each period's income statements next to each other, it's possible to do what is called a horizontal analysis—an assessment of changes in each item. By calculating the percentage of change between periods for each item, you can track trends, which may indicate a change in your costs or revenues, and can identify the sources of that change. Horizontal analyses are great for tracking changes over time and are often described in terms of YOY (year over year), QOQ (quarter over quarter) or MOM (month over month). By contrast, a vertical analysis includes any calculations of ratios between two or more elements in a single financial statement. For example, in an income statement, you might want to calculate the percentage of your total income spent on operational expenses or, even more specifically, your mortgage. Whereas horizontal analyses track changes over time, vertical analyses assess the composition of your finances. Despite the fancy names, there's really nothing complicated about them—they are just calculations of percentages, performed by dividing one value by another, just like you learned at elementary school.

Horizontal analysis: An assessment that calculates financial changes over time.

Vertical analysis: An assessment that calculates the composition of financial allocations.

BUDGET

The reason it's necessary to understand the income statement before we discuss budgeting is that your budget will include information from your income statement. Recall from earlier in this chapter that a budget is used as a planning tool for how to distribute your money in future. So, before you begin budgeting, you must know the amount of money you have and how you are currently spending it. This makes budgeting very similar to doing a horizontal analysis of your income statement *prior* to the next period, rather than in hindsight, as would be typical with the income statement.

An effective budget will tell you three things about each item:

1. The total amount of money allocated to each item
2. The percentage each item comprises of the total available money for the period
3. The cumulative percentage of these items of the total available money for the period.

Generally this begins with the total amount of income you have available during the period. Note that we are not referring to the total amount you intend to spend, because even putting money in your savings is an allocation of your available resources; so, include your entire gross sales for the period at the top.

Disposable income

Once you have determined how much your total income is going to be for the period, calculate how much you are going to have to pay in taxes for the period, and subtract that amount. Since taxes are generally assessed on an annual or quarterly basis, calculating your taxes at this stage will be an estimate based on your expected annual income, divided across periods. It's easiest to divide the value equally, but if you want to get a little fancy with your math, you can use a weighted average based on your productivity for the period. In any case, once you have subtracted your taxes from your total income, you are left with something called your disposable income. Since the government always gets their share, this means that part of your income is already accounted for before you formally spend it.

REMEMBER THIS!!! Your disposable income is all the income you have earned, after tax, which you are legally allowed to do with as you like.

Discretionary income

There are many things which people need to survive: food, drink, housing, clothing, some types of insurance, a minimum degree of transportation and so forth. These are not expenses which you are legally obligated to incur, as when calculating disposable income, but this is money you are obligated to spend if you enjoy surviving and would like to continue to do so, at least into the immediate future. Generally this includes all COGS items from your income statement, as well as other necessities from your operational expenses.

Once you have subtracted all these items from your disposable income, the value that remains is known as your 'discretionary income'—the total amount of money you have remaining to spend on luxuries and entertainment, and/or to allocate to investments and savings. As with your income statement, the individual items should be listed (or groups of similar items clustered into broad categories such as 'entertainment spending' or 'equities investments').

If you have multiple savings accounts or multiple types of investments, this should be noted. In particular, if you keep a separate account for retirement investments, list it separately.

When budgeting your discretionary income for the period, the order in which you list the items doesn't change anything, but organizing the budgeted items by priority can help you to assess more easily which expenditures are more flexible than others. This often puts retirement accounts at the top of discretionary income, because it's beneficial to calculate the amount of money you will need to retire, as well as how much you will need to set aside each period in order to reach that goal (procedures which will be discussed in greater detail in chapter 9). Generally speaking, it's prudent to strive towards the goal of spending as little as possible on items near the bottom while still meeting your needs, and to find ways to reduce this amount so that a greater percentage of your total assets can be budgeted towards things you value more greatly near the top of the budget.

Since budgets are planning tools, it's very possible that the actual amount you allocate to each item will be different from what you planned. This is reflected in the difference between the estimated value and the observed value—estimated value being the amount you planned to allocate to that item, and the observed value being the amount you actually allocated during that period. The difference between these two values will tell you how to alter your future planning. Sometimes you will need to explore ways to allocate fewer assets to a particular item, such as by decreasing the amount of money you spend; while other times you may need to plan on allocating greater assets to a particular item, such as putting more assets into your retirement account if your investments have been underperforming; and other times you will end up spending less on a particular item, allowing you to find better ways to use that money in the future.

Discretionary income: The amount of remaining income after all legal and subsistence expenses are paid.

Estimated value: The monetary value that is predicted based on trends and/or calculations.

Observed value: The monetary value that is actually experienced.

Have a go at putting your budget together using the table overleaf, using the 'Item 1' and 'Item 2' rows for your essential expenses (your COGS items) and adding in rows as needed. Note that both the top and bottom cumulative percentages are 100. Your available assets figure is the total value being distributed, so clearly it is 100 per cent of itself; other percentages listed will eventually sum to the total available assets, which is why 'Luxuries'—or whatever you include at the bottom of your budget—is also 100 per cent.

For each item listed, if there is a difference in the estimated and observed values, you have a couple of options on how to respond. First, you can roll over the difference into the next period: if you have a little extra left over after not allocating as much as you planned to a particular item, then the next period you can increase the amount budgeted to that item by the amount of the difference. Say, for example, your travel expenditures are higher one month than expected—you can maintain the rest of your budget the same and simply reduce the amount budgeted to transportation next month. This is best utilized on items that tend to vary from period to period, in order to help compensate for average variability over time.

The problem with this approach is that if the difference continues consistently over time, you will be forced to resort to the second

	Estimated value	Percentage of total	Cumulative percentage	Observed value	Difference
Available assets	$XX.xx	100%	100%	$XX.xx	X%
Taxes	$XX.xx	X%	X%	$XX.xx	X%
Disposable income	$XX.xx	X%	–	$XX.xx	X%
Item 1	$XX.xx	X%	X%	$XX.xx	X%
Item 2	$XX.xx	X%	X%	$XX.xx	X%
Discretionary income	$XX.xx	X%	–	$XX.xx	X%
Retirement	$XX.xx	X%	X%	$XX.xx	X%
Investments	$XX.xx	X%	X%	$XX.xx	X%
Savings	$XX.xx	X%	X%	$XX.xx	X%
Luxuries	$XX.xx	X%	100%	$XX.xx	X%

option—recording the difference from somewhere else. Theoretically, you can continue to roll over differences in estimated and observed budget items indefinitely, but all the extra money (or lack thereof) must go somewhere. It will be attributed either to one of your accounts or one of your expenditures. Let's return to your rolled-over travel costs: if transportation is consistently higher than expected every month, then the growing difference will need to be funded either by spending less on something else or by reducing the amount allocated to your savings and/or investments. Remember that a budget is a planning tool; so, even if you pull the money from future budgets, you are still spending the money now, and this will be reflected in your total assets as you use them.

THINK ABOUT IT

Budgets help you plan for the future, while income statements report on the past; information from past income statements helps shape our future budgets, while the manner in which we budget our money affects what happens on the income statement. The problem that many people have while budgeting is that they attempt to combine these two things into one report that neither plans nor reports well, leading to poor execution of financial management. It's a little more work to do both, but there's a reason all major corporations, non-profits, entrepreneurs, investors and financial experts do it this way—it's more informative and more useful in managing how much money you have to work with and how you utilize it.

– 3 –

BANKING

People tend to treat banks as places to put their money in order to keep it safe, opening an account so that someone else is responsible for the storage of their earnings. Banks were never intended to be glorified storage units, though, and there are a number of financial services and products available to the general public that can accomplish the same goal, but which also provide additional benefits.

Banks play a vital role in both your personal finances and global economies, but in order to reap the benefits of what they have to offer, it's necessary to understand exactly *what* banks are offering. In this chapter we will explore the original role of banks as depository institutions, the other types of depository institutions which have been incorporated into the global banking infrastructure, and how you can use these services to help manage your finances.

DEPOSITORY INSTITUTIONS

There are various types of depository institutions, each with its own subtly unique traits, which have all come to be known colloquially as 'banks'. It's not a completely unfair evolution of casual language, since all depository institutions serve the same primary functions, but there are slight differences between each of them which must be considered when managing your finances, since these differences have far-reaching implications.

Commercial banks

Banks are the largest type of depository institution. They function as intermediaries between people who have money that they don't need right away and people who need money. Banks do this by taking deposits from the first group of customers and issuing a portion as loans to the second group. Banks charge debtors interest as their primary source of income, and offer a smaller rate of interest on accounts in order to attract deposits; they profit off the difference between the two, which is known as 'the spread'.

The role of banks is critical to the overall functionality of the global economy because without them it would be extremely difficult for lenders and borrowers to figure out the logistics of legal contract and enforcement and to find borrowers who want to borrow less money than the lender has available for a shorter period of time than the lender intends to lend it. When thousands or millions of potential lenders all pool their funds together in a bank, however, even when accounting for withdrawals, there is consistently enough money available to make large, long-term loans. And, since all these people are gathered at a single place with their funds, borrowers know exactly where to go to apply for a loan and do not have to work hard to find lenders. Banks, then, function as an intermediary that increases global financial mobility.

However, actual bank operations often deviate from their original purpose—many banks now charge for bank accounts rather than offering interest to their depositors, fund management often lacks proper handling of risk (discussed in chapter 7), and banks often come under fire for unscrupulous practices. As with anything you do, remember to shop around and explore your options, not just with a variety of banks, but also with other depository institutions.

Credit unions

After the banking scandals that followed the 2008 financial collapse, many people discovered credit unions for the first time and a huge migration of people from banks to credit unions ensued. Like banks, credit unions make money primarily by issuing loans at a higher interest rate than the amount they pay depositors, but unlike banks, credit unions don't treat deposits as loans—they treat them as a share of ownership in the operations of the credit union. In other words, when you deposit money at a credit union, you own a share of the operations of that credit union and earn a rate of return that is consistent with its earnings.

Members of the credit union vote on its directors, as opposed to shareholders or owners voting, as with a bank. Credit unions are also non-profit, which tends to result in higher-quality services for members than are available at banks, but their smaller size limits the range of services available.

Savings institutions

Savings institutions go by a wide variety of names, depending on the specific focus of each: 'savings and loan', 'building society', 'savings bank', 'savings association', etc. Like credit unions, savings institutions are member-owned, and depositors earn a rate of return on their accounts that is consistent with the investing activities of the institution. They differ, however, in that each savings institution specializes in a particular type of lending, such as mortgages. The distinction between different types of savings institutions, and even between savings institutions and credit unions, is often one of legal technicality rather than operational difference.

The world has seen a sharp decline in the number of savings institutions as the broader scope of banks and credit unions not only attracts more customers, but also shields them from the real estate volatility experienced by savings institutions.

TYPES OF ACCOUNTS

Savings accounts

Savings accounts are very simple and have low, fixed interest rates, which means that most people use them as storage. Whatever money people haven't either spent or put into their retirement accounts tends to get put into a savings account, and since the person doesn't have any immediate plans for it, the money tends to automatically default to entertainment or luxury spending. While entertainment and luxury are necessary things to maintain good morale and high levels of motivation, it's a bad habit to simply default to these with any money for which you haven't yet accounted in other ways.

It's also a bad idea to simply let money accumulate in the savings account, because you could really be doing other things with it that earn you a greater rate of income than the super-low interest rates earned by savings accounts.

Instead, think of savings accounts as a tool to manage your working capital—the money you set aside for the regular fluctuations in your available cash. Every month, perhaps every week, the amount of money you have will vary depending on when you get paid, when your bills are due, unforeseen circumstances, etc. Even though you may not be using your money right away, you will need it imminently, and you will likely want to keep a little extra, just in case you run out of funds unexpectedly. This is the money you want to keep in your savings account, where it will earn a little bit of interest until you are ready to use it, but which doesn't earn enough interest to warrant keeping more money than you need in it.

If your transaction account, discussed next, earns an interest rate equal to or higher than available savings accounts, then it's completely unnecessary to have a savings account at all, except if your country has special types of savings accounts which are given preferential tax status.

Transaction accounts

Whether you know them as 'current', 'checking' or (the more generic) 'transaction' accounts, these bank accounts are intended to make your money easily accessible for the purpose of making payments. These accounts can be accessed not only by direct withdrawal, but also by paper cheque, debit card and electronic transfers. The bills you pay will most likely be funded from your transaction account.

The high levels of activity on transaction accounts mean that the amount of money in these accounts tends to be extremely variable, and so they often yield little or no interest, or even have charges attached to them. Rarely, however, especially among credit unions, transaction accounts will yield interest as high as 3 per cent. If your account does have an interest rate, if possible, try to pay your bills at the last minute, using auto-pay options if they are available to minimize any chance of errors resulting in late payments, and collect on money you are owed as quickly as possible in order to maximize the amount of funds on which you are earning interest.

Timed accounts

There are some types of accounts in which you deposit funds with a guarantee that you won't withdraw them for a set period of time.

The increased amount of certainty associated with these accounts permits banks to offer depositors higher rates of interest. Of course, you have access to your money if it's absolutely necessary, but generally that will incur financial penalties that prevent you from keeping the entirety of your earned interest. Certificates of deposit (CDs) are a form of timed account that are sold at a minimum value or in fixed increments.

Money market accounts

Variable-rate savings, or 'money market', accounts are for rich people. These function just like savings accounts, except the interest rates they yield vary depending on market interest rates, which means they are treated like an investment into the domestic currency. These accounts require an extremely high balance, making them generally inappropriate for most people. Since the amount of working capital you are likely to have will not exceed that minimum balance, other investment options are likely to be a more viable choice.

Brokerage accounts

These are the accounts used when investing, which will be discussed in greater detail in chapter 6. These accounts function like a waiting area for funds that haven't yet been invested, but which the owner intends to invest.

Retirement accounts

There are several different types of retirement account, which will be discussed in greater detail in chapter 9. They are all special types of brokerage account which are granted special tax status, but the exact tax benefits depend on the type of account. These accounts are intended to be used only for retirement savings, and the special tax status is lost on any funds within the account that are used for any reason other than that specified by the laws in your country.

Joint accounts

A joint account can be any of the above types of account but is owned by more than one person. This is particularly common between spouses.

Flexible-spending accounts

A flex-spend account, as it is colloquially known, is a type of temporary account offered by a person's employer as a perk. The owner of the account decides how much of their regular wages should be directed to this account, and they are allowed to spend it on qualifying expenses without being subject to income tax. In other words, whatever you spend your flex money on will not count towards the income taxes you pay. Not all expenses count, however—generally just things which improve your ability to work, such as health care or child care. As noted, these accounts are temporary, or at least your ability to use funds within it is—these are 'use it or lose it' accounts, which means that if you don't use it within a specified period of time, you lose the perk and the cycle starts anew.

ACCOUNTING

Accounting, or accounts, refers to the written organization of financial information. So, you may have your bank accounts, but you might also have money set aside to save for a vacation, which you call the Vacation Fund account. Every time you pull money from your savings account to put it into the Vacation Fund, the Vacation Fund gets a positive value entry, and the savings account gets a negative value entry, because you are reducing the value of your savings account to increase the value of the Vacation Fund, and both transactions must be recorded.

This is the core of something called double-entry accounting. When you are keeping track of everything, every single transaction you record has an equivalent but opposite transaction—every positive must also have a negative. Even on payday, when you get your wages, the increase in the value of your bank account comes with a decrease in the amount of money owed to you—known as 'wages earned'. The sum of all transactions should then always equal zero, and if they do not, there's an error somewhere in your finances that needs to be found. Double-entry accounting is used to ensure that the movement of all assets is recorded, rather than just the values of the accounts.

KEY TERM

Double-entry accounting: A system of financial record keeping that ties changes in the value of one account to an opposite change in value to another account.

Although double-entry accounting has a lot of specific methods and rules that have evolved over years of use at major corporations and financial institutions, the average person does not need a system that is so sophisticated. So long as you record the changes in value, both positive and negative, tracking asset movement in a way that makes sense to you, then it's a successful system. For example, you may give each account its own page in your books and then record the dated increases and decreases in value as a list, and that may be enough. If you are an investor, entrepreneur or business owner, you may want to purchase an introductory accounting book to help you learn more sophisticated methods of record keeping, or you may even want to purchase accounting software to assist.

FUTURE VALUE

If you know how much money is in your bank account and the rate of interest your account earns (and if you don't, go ask your teller), then you can calculate exactly how much your account will be worth at any point in the future, known as its 'future value'. Future value is also useful for calculating how much you will earn on fixed-income investments (discussed in chapter 6) and how much you will have to pay on debts (discussed in chapter 5). These calculations of future value are useful in any context in which you want to know how much an interest-generating asset will be worth at some point in the future, regardless of whether it's a bank account or any other type of asset. There are a few, common types of interest rates used, each with their own specific method of determining future value.

Simple interest = $P(1 + r)^t$

If your bank account pays interest just on the principal balance, or you withdraw any interest on income you earn before getting paid again, then you are earning simple interest. Simple interest means that no matter how much money you make over time, you are still just earning income on the original balance.

KEY TERMS

Future value: The monetary value of an investment or account at any future time.

Simple interest: The accrual of interest income or payments at a constant rate.

In this formula, P is your principal balance—the amount of money you put into your account (or the original amount of your loan or the value of a bond investment, etc.). The value r is the rate of interest you earn, but remember to include it as a decimal instead of a percentage. So, if your bank account earns 1 per cent interest, the r value will be 0.01, and if your bank account earns 50 per cent interest, the r value will be 0.5. The value t is the length of time for which you want to know the future value, measured in years.

Consider an example of a bank account with $100 that earns 10 per cent interest and is kept open for five years. Using the formula of simple interest = $P(1 + r)^t$, the calculation would be $100(1 + 0.1)^5$, which equals a total value of $161.05. That means that in five years you will have earned $61.05 on your initial investment of $100.

USEFUL TIP: If you tried the calculation yourself and got a value of 16,105,100,000, remember to add the values in the parentheses *first*, and then calculate the exponent (*t*) before multiplying by the principal (*P*).

Compound interest = $P(1 + [r/n])^{nt}$

More often than not, bank accounts earn compound interest, which means that you will earn interest on both the principal and the interest you have earned. Say your account is compounded monthly: the amount of interest income you earn on the account will be based on the amount of money that's in the account at the end of each month, rather than on the principal alone. This changes the calculation slightly, but it's just a variation of simple interest rather than a whole new process.

P is still the principal, r is still rate, and t is still time. The difference is that we are now including the value n, which is the number of times compounding per year. So, if we have an account with a principal balance of $100 which earns 10 per cent interest that compounds monthly and is kept open for five years, the calculation would be $100(1 + [0.1/12])^{12*5}$. Since the account compounds monthly, it compounds twelve times per year; so, at the end of five years the account balance will be \$164.53, which means you have earned \$64.53 on your initial investment of \$100. Compare that to simple interest, wherein you only earned \$61.05—the compounding account earned \$3.48 more over the course of five years.

Continuously compounding interest = Pe^{rt}

There is a special type of compound interest known as 'continuously compounding interest', which means that the account continues to compound constantly, rather than being calculated at regular intervals. This is possible thanks to the value *e*, which is a mathematical constant equal to about 2.72. Like the number π (pi, 3.141592 . . .), *e* is an irrational number with no end, which is why it's always rounded. It is used to calculate growth rates of things which grow exponentially, like continuously compounding interest. Looking at the example of a continuously compounding account with a principal balance of \$100 that earns 10 per cent interest over a period of five years, the calculation would be $100e^{0.1*5}$, giving us a value of \$164.92. This is \$0.39 higher than the account which compounded monthly.

– 4 –

MAJOR PURCHASES

Not everything you buy is an investment. You are not investing in new furniture, or a boat, or necessarily even a car. An investment is something you buy with the expectation that it will generate more income for you than you spent. Your house, then, meets the qualification of being an investment, since real estate increases in value, on average.

The vast majority of everything you will buy is a purchase, not an investment. A purchase includes anything you buy with the expectation of its losing value, including all basic consumption. It is only in rare cases that things like cars will actually increase in value, and these are typically older, collector's models, rather than new ones. While purchases do constitute a financial loss, they are also entirely unavoidable, being necessary for survival, function and morale. Most of the purchases you make will be small things which require little attention—at most, some simple comparison shopping and coupon use.

There are a handful of common purchases, however, which are comparatively immense and will play total havoc on your finances if you are not careful, such as vehicles, education/training and some types of medical treatments. In this chapter, we will explore ways to integrate these purchases into your financial management strategy to ensure not only that you get the best value possible, but also to ensure your financial stability itself.

KEY TERMS

Investment: Any expenditure made with the expectation of increased value over time.

Purchase: Any expenditure made with the expectation of lost value over time.

LIST YOUR NEEDS

Before you even begin considering the kind of purchase you want to make, it's vital that you articulate exactly what you need. Define and list the exact problems you are facing which you believe a purchase will resolve and describe the traits that must be present in order to successfully achieve that goal. In other words, write the exact things your purchase must offer in order to meet your needs. You may find that there are substitutes for your intended purchase which provide greater utility for you or which meet your needs as well but at a lower price. You may determine that the purchase you are thinking of making actually doesn't fulfil your needs at all, or that the price doesn't justify meeting needs of a frivolous nature.

In order to help you in this process, ask yourself the following questions, ensuring you write specific answers to each:

- How did you get by without the purchase until now?
- In what ways will the purchase change your life?
- Do consumer reviews state that the purchase does what it claims? Check on the internet and in consumer magazines or industry publications, and ask people you know who have bought the same thing.
- What alternatives to the purchase are available which will also meet your needs?

- Can your finances handle the expense?
- Did you recently get a financial windfall (e.g., inheritance, winnings, tax return), and would you have made this purchase without it?
- What are three reasons why you don't need the purchase?

Asking these questions will help not only to guarantee you are making the best purchase possible for your unique circumstances, but also to avoid *buyer's remorse*—a state in which you buy something as a result of excitement and novelty, only to wish later that you hadn't spent the money.

ESTIMATE VALUE

If you have determined that the purchase is absolutely necessary, it's time to do some research. For major purchases, the cost of making a mistake regarding the fair market price or the price of debt financing, or of failing to follow up after your purchase, can easily make a very serious difference in your finances.

Before you even begin shopping for the best place to make your purchase, establish the fair market value. Unlike small items, you can typically negotiate on price for major purchases; generally assume that the asking price is higher than the fair market price. Your best defence against paying too much for a thing is knowing its true value. The internet is an amazing resource for this, as are consumer magazines and industry publications. It's also prudent to research the value of comparable products: new vs. used, different makes, models or years of production, different features offered, owner-sold vs. dealer-sold, and even the same thing bought from different locations.

It's even possible that market prices will experience seasonal fluctuations, making it prudent to wait, if the difference in price will be greater than any costs incurred as a result of waiting the extra time. The more you know about the influences on market price, the more effective you will be during price negotiations.

Market price isn't the only thing to consider to estimate the financial value of a major purchase. The purchase may actually replace other expenses you currently incur; for example, purchasing a car will reduce or eliminate your transportation costs associated with taking the bus, though whether one is better value than the other will depend on the individual person.

Most major purchases also have a resale or scrap value. Resale value is the price at which you will be able to sell the product after x number of years of ownership, regaining some of your initial cost. The scrap value is the price at which you can sell your purchase once you have completely consumed its usable life, when you are merely trying to sell it for salvageable parts and materials.

Since most major purchases are too expensive for a person to afford in a single payment, debt financing is used, such as a mortgage or a car loan. The interest rates you will pay on that loan (a topic discussed in greater detail in chapter 3) force you to pay a higher total price for your product than it is actually worth, so this should be avoided if at all possible. All these things play a role in the price you will pay for a product and must be weighed against the benefits you will receive from its use.

Once you have chosen a specific item to purchase, inspect it to ensure that it is exactly what you want and in good condition. Despite your best efforts, you will never be 100 per cent certain that nothing will go wrong. It is for this reason that people invented warranties, which are promises to repair and/or replace a major purchase that becomes defective within a specified period of time after the initial purchase. Often, specific types of damage are excluded, such as water damage on a mobile phone or damage from misuse. Sometimes warranties must be purchased for an additional fee and sometimes they can be extended for an additional fee. For major purchases, extended warranties are generally included, but, as with anything, you must consider the price of the extended warranty compared to the cost and likelihood of repair/replacement. A particular type of warranty helps to protect you against price fluctuations, known as a 'price protection plan'. You may find yourself in a scenario wherein you make a very large purchase, only to discover that the price drops significantly the next day. Price protection plans guarantee that if the market price of the purchase drops suddenly during a predetermined period of time after the initial purchase, you will receive a refund in the amount of the difference.

KEY TERMS

Resale value: The price at which an item can be resold after a period of ownership.

Scrap value: The price at which an item can be sold for scrap or parts after its useful life has been consumed.

Warranty: A contractual guarantee by a manufacturer or seller to incur some or all of the financial risk associated with the chance of faulty or damaged products.

BUDGET

Now that you have determined what you are going to pay for your purchase, double-check that you can afford it. It is, of course, best to pay for your purchase in advance, paying for it in its entirety at the time of purchase, rather than buying the item and slowly paying for it afterward, including interest payments that make the purchase more expensive. Save little by little before the purchase and avoid the interest payments. Create a row in your monthly budget (see p. 28) that sets aside a fixed amount of money consistently until you have enough, and this will keep you from overpaying.

It's easy to say 'save your money', but sometimes a major expenditure must be made urgently, requiring you to borrow the money. If that's the case, then remember that you must account not just for the cost of the purchase, but also the cost of your interest payments (discussed in greater detail in chapter 3). Establish exactly how much you will have to pay each month and determine where those funds will come from. If you are allocating money to debt repayments, then that's money which is not being used for something else; so, what aspect of your finances will be getting less attention? Are you able to allocate enough money to this repayment without defaulting on other costs? These questions can be sobering in a moment when marketers and salespeople would have you focus on the excitement—whereas the excitement is just a bit of fun, your finances will shape the rest of your life.

REDUCE PRICE

It is prudent to do everything you can to negotiate on price, as even a small percentage reduction will result in substantial savings when purchasing things of high value. It's in the nature of large-ticket items that the price tends to be negotiable; you are given individual attention from people who are frequently paid at least partially on a commission of what they sell, and who work for a company with enough autonomy to adjust their profit margin on each sale, if needed. This purchase will have a significant impact on your future finances, and you will likely have this purchase for an extended period of time, so take advantage of these points of negotiation.

REMEMBER THIS!!!

Your best tool in this case is knowledge. Research the fair market value, average profit margin and average sales commission (or even apply for a job as a salesperson to determine with certainty their sales compensation structure), and check competitors, private sellers, seasonal fluctuations and comparable alternative brands and models. If any of these provides an opportunity to convince them to reduce their price, use it to your advantage. Do remember, though, that a good negotiation ends with all parties pleased with the result, or else the negotiation will fail. So, explain to them what you intend and how they will benefit from it, emphasizing the big win-win.

If a previously owned purchase is not an option, consider purchasing the demonstration model. Other than real estate, all common major purchases begin to lose value instantly; vehicles are notorious for losing an immense amount of their value the moment you sign the contract. Demo models are still new but cannot be sold as such because they have been sampled by potential buyers, and so their selling price is significantly reduced without a meaningful reduction in the functional life of the purchase.

If you intend to finance your purchase using a loan, first read chapter 5, then contact one of the major credit bureaus to get a copy of your credit report. The interest rate you will be charged for the loan is based heavily on your credit history, so you will want to ensure there are no errors on your report which may result in higher interest charges than necessary. Major credit bureaus provide credit reports for free or for a small fee, depending on where you live. They are simple to read, listing your current and past debts and other credit activity; so, if you see any errors in the report, or anything unfamiliar, call them to challenge it. It may mean a very significant difference in the rate you are offered on a loan.

Finally, remember that the lowest price is not necessarily the best value. Sometimes the cheaper option has a lower lifespan, higher cost of maintenance or otherwise does not fulfil your needs as effectively. This is not intended to be a justification for spending extra money on frivolous features and unnecessary brand markups, but a true assessment of how long the purchase will last and what costs will be associated with it.

After the purchase, if you find any problems, be sure to keep detailed records, collect evidence if necessary (e.g., photos, maintenance records, repair invoices, emergency response statements, etc.) and follow up with the seller. It may be appropriate for them to repair, replace or refund your purchase, but do be aware of their rights as well: you can't consume a large portion of the useful life of the purchase and expect your money back.

– 5 –

DEBT MANAGEMENT

It may come as a surprise to learn that not all debt is bad, and it may be even more surprising to find out that some debt can be a good thing. Consider a situation in which you have the opportunity to earn 10 per cent per year on an investment. You don't have the money, but you have the opportunity to borrow the money at only 5 per cent interest per year. That means you must pay 5 per cent of the principal you borrow each year, but the way in which you have invested that same money has earned you a consistent 10 per cent of the same amount each year. Sure, those interest payments will stop you from earning your full 10 per cent annually, but you are still going to make money by using that debt rather than lose it, as you might expect.

We already explored how to calculate interest rates in chapter 3 (see p. 39), so now we are more concerned with the nature of debt and how to manage it. Debt management isn't merely about paying off your debts and refusing to incur more of them—if it were that easy, this chapter would be little more than an introductory paragraph. Instead, we will explore the different types of debt and how to turn bad debt into good debt, but first we need to know where to apply for debt.

DEBT INSTITUTIONS

Debt institutions include any organizations which offer loans to borrowers who both apply and qualify for the particular type of loan issued by each institution. There are a variety of types.

Depository institutions

There is a lot of overlap between debt institutions and depository institutions, the latter of which were discussed in chapter 3 (see p. 31). In fact, most times that you apply for a loan, you will actually be going to a depository institution to do it—loans are, after all, the primary source of revenues for these organizations. They offer a wide variety of loans for both personal and business purposes, all funded by the money which their customers deposit.

Sales financing institutions

Many non-financial companies offer their own loans to customers. This is particularly common among companies that sell expensive items which a customer may need to pay for over time, such as vehicles, furniture, electronics, home repairs and so forth. Sometimes, the companies that sell these things offer the loans themselves; sometimes a private third-party company that specializes in sales financing offers the service for them. Any financing you see available for a purchase is a type of loan.

Credit institutions

By far the most common type of credit debt is the credit card. Credit cards are generally offered by companies associated with major banks, or by the banks themselves, but they are also offered by other organizations. They offer to individuals and companies lines of credit, which are unique types of ongoing, open-ended loans that are available for use at the borrower's discretion.

KEY TERM **Lines of credit:** A type of loan in which money can be continuously borrowed and repaid at the discretion of the borrower.

Payday lenders

These companies offer extremely short-term loans to people who intend to pay them back in full the next time they get paid. These lenders charge tremendously high fees and take advantage of people who struggle week to week and generally resort to these lenders out of desperation. In the world of finance, they are considered to be legal loan sharks.

COMMON TYPES OF LOANS

In seeking debt, the type of loan for which you apply depends entirely on your intended use of funds. Each type of loan has a distinct purpose, and once you have identified the type of loan you need, you will likely have several different options in interest rates and repayment periods. Inadvertently incurring destructive debt is one of the most common mistakes that lead people into financial ruin, so make sure you know what you are getting before you sign any agreements.

Student debt

Students who pay for tuition themselves are often required to take out loans to be able to afford the cost. In accepting these loans, borrowers assume that the long-term difference in their income potential will be greater than the amount of interest they accrue over the course of their university life, often including cost of living expenses.

Student debt is an increasingly controversial topic in many countries, where tuition rates increase at a much faster rate than the rate of income increases, even for university graduates. People argue that these debts merely entrap young people during what will most likely be the most financially volatile time of their life. In some countries, student loans are subsidized by the government while the student is at university, so that the loans don't accrue interest; in other countries, these loans are guaranteed by the government so that lenders face little or no risk of default, which is typically made legally impossible.

Mortgages

Mortgages are loans offered to people using their house as collateral. Most frequently, this means giving funds to home buyers for the purchase of a house, but it's also possible to put a lien on your house as collateral (which means the lender gets your house if you default) in order to fund other large expenses. These loans are often called home equity lines of credit (HELOC) and allow you to borrow against the amount of equity on your home (see p. 73). These are typically long-term loans with a repayment period of either 15 or 30 years, and lenders frequently also offer escrow services, which means they charge additional funds that are used to pay for home insurance, property taxes or both, at no additional cost. Mortgages can be fixed rate, variable rate or hybrid rate (discussed later in this chapter).

KEY TERMS

Lien: Legal right to ownership of property by a lender in the case of default.

Home equity lines of credit (HELOC): A line of credit that uses home equity as collateral.

Escrow: Custody through a third party until a specified condition has been met.

Consumer loans

Consumer loans include any sort of financing you use to pay for your purchases. These are typically short-term, fixed-rate loans and often offer perks like 0 per cent interest for x number of months, though larger purchases such as cars have loans which last several years.

Danger debt

There are two types of loans which every person should think about very carefully before even applying—credit cards and payday loans. Both of these types of loans are extremely predatory. Payday loans have extremely high fixed rates and heavy penalties, despite being typically borrowed for only a few days, targeting those who are so desperate for money they cannot wait until the end of the week. These loans have become renowned for decimating a person's finances and credit. Credit cards, by contrast, can appear to have attractive rates at first, but that can change dramatically, without reason or warning, and frequently does. People are often attracted to the ease, convenience and recorded history associated with a credit card (all things which can be found just as easily in a debit card), and over time they get lax with their repayments. They fall into the trap of making minimum payments, leading to overpayment for basic consumer goods, increasing amounts of risk and, all too often, total financial collapse. Before you underestimate the risk associated with credit cards, remember that they were a primary contributor to the Great Depression of the 1930s.

Consolidation loans

If you have several different types of loans, it may be worth considering applying for a consolidation loan. Simply, you use the money from your consolidation loan to pay the remaining balance on all your other loans so that you are paying only one loan instead of many.

This has several benefits. First, when you are paying back fewer loans, your total monthly payments tend to decrease, since you are paying back an equivalent total balance but to fewer lenders, requiring lower total monthly minimum payments. Second, loan consolidation can, but cannot be guaranteed to, lower interest rates. This is due to the fact that loan consolidation makes existing debt easier to repay and, therefore, lower risk to the lender than the borrower's current circumstances. Loan consolidation can also help your credit rating (discussed in more detail later in this chapter). Although a consolidation loan itself may actually have a negative impact on your credit rating, its reduction in the number of loans you have, when done properly, will ensure you don't continue to miss or delay payments.

It is critical to remember, though, that loan consolidation could mean you will end up paying more total money back than you otherwise would. Since you are paying back an equivalent total balance—but over a longer period of time—you will continue to accrue and repay interest payments for a longer time as well.

Refinancing

Similar to a consolidation loan, refinancing is another option for using new debt to repay old debt. Specifically, refinancing means that you apply for a loan that is almost identical to an existing loan but with a lower interest rate, and then use the lower-rate loan to pay your higher-rate loan. Let's say, for example, you have a 30-year mortgage at 6 per cent interest, and the market for mortgages drops to 3 per cent interest; you can apply for a new 30-year mortgage on the exact same house but at the lower rate. The end result is that you reduce your total monthly payments.

Be careful, though: this is most effective when you still have a lot of time remaining on your repayment period. If you have only five years remaining on a 30-year mortgage and then refinance, you are going to be making interest payments at that lower rate, but for an extra 25 years, which means you will end up paying more for the refinance than it's worth. Refinancing is best for those people who were approved for a loan immediately before a sudden drop in interest rates.

Fixed, variable and hybrid rates

All types of loans, including those discussed in this chapter, can be either fixed rate, variable rate or a hybrid of the two. A fixed-rate loan has an interest rate which will never change, so you always know how much you will have to repay. A variable-rate loan, also known as an 'adjustable-rate loan', has an interest rate which will change.

There are a variety of different types of variable rate loan, such as those that vary with your income, those that vary with some economic indicator such as a stock index, those that vary in predetermined ways over time (e.g., reduced or 0 per cent interest rates during the first few months or years of the loan) or, really, just about anything else you can imagine. Loan rates have gotten very imaginative as lenders try to attract new borrowers with sales gimmicks or by appealing to legitimate niche needs. Of the more exotic of these loans is the hybrid-rate loan, which includes elements of both fixed and variable rates. Sometimes, this means that a loan will be fixed for a period of time and then vary afterward, or that a loan will vary in its rate but with a fixed maximum or minimum rate, or that your rate will be fixed so long as your annual income does not exceed a certain value.

Fixed-rate loan: A loan that charges a constant rate of interest.

Variable-rate loan: A loan that charges a rate of interest which is subject to change.

Hybrid-rate loan: A loan that has elements of both a fixed-rate and variable-rate loan.

REPAYING DEBT

The core of debt management is knowing which debts to pay and when to pay them. For many people, this sounds counterintuitive because they are so used to simply paying on a schedule that has been determined for them, or even just making the minimum monthly payments on their loan. While this can be a great approach if all your debt is already in its optimal position—something more common among financial professionals than anyone—you might find that, once you understand a few basic debt management strategies, you can improve your long-term financial potential immensely.

The simplest approach to debt management is to pay the debts which accrue the greatest interest costs first. This means that if you are going to pay higher than the minimum payments on any of your loans, it should be the one that is costing you the most. Maybe that's the loan with the highest interest rate, or maybe that's the loan with an extremely high balance. Some loans accrue interest costs based on the remaining balance rather than the principal; in which case, it may be prudent to pay down your biggest loan, even if it's not your highest-rate loan. The easiest way to determine which loan is costing you the most is to multiply the interest rate by either the balance or the principal, depending on the loan.

Another easy strategy to improve your loan structure is to push all your debts to your lowest-interest loans, known as 'debt reorganization'. In other words, if you have multiple loans with different interest rates, then by paying your high-interest loans using funds from your low-interest loans, you can reduce your total costs. This is a particularly common option with open-ended loans like lines of credit, which have no fixed duration. Reorganization is unique from debt consolidation, which is another valid option for debt repayment (noted earlier in this chapter), in that the goal is not to limit the number of loans outstanding, but rather to lower the interest rates on your loans even if there are still several of them. Debt consolidation also tends to be a one-time event, consolidating all the loans into one, all at once, while debt reorganization can be as long a process as necessary, moving a little debt at a time as your maximum limits on low-interest loans become available through gradual repayment. Reorganization also has the benefit over consolidation in that it does not create a new debt that will necessarily extend the total life of your loans. Instead, you decrease your monthly payments by decreasing your interest rates, rather than by extending the duration of your payments.

KEY TERM

Debt reorganization: A change in the value and costs of several loans through planned repayment strategies.

Be careful to note, however, that paying debt with other debt is not always debt reorganization. If you find that you are only able to make your minimum payments on some debts by using funds from other debts, then it's time to jump to a different set of strategies (found in this chapter under the 'Last Resorts' heading).

Remember that interest is not just something you pay—you can also earn it, if you invest your money. Most people have income-generating assets like a bank account or investments, as well as debt. This changes the dynamic of your debt strategy. The difference between constructive and destructive debt is that constructive debt maintains interest rates which are lower than the income you are generating using that money, while destructive debt has interest rates which are higher, causing you to lose money. When you have income-generating assets (discussed in chapter 6), the question is no longer about which debt is the most expensive—although that should certainly still be a consideration—but about how you can allocate your resources in a way that maintains the highest level of income. You still need to repay your debts, regardless of how constructive they are, but you can choose whether to make your minimum payments if your debt has lower interest rates than the income you are generating by keeping your money in an investment. If your debt has higher interest rates than the amount of income you are generating by keeping that money, then pay that debt in its entirety as quickly as possible, because you are losing money.

KEY TERMS

Constructive debt: Debt in which the money is used to generate income or wealth at a higher rate than the interest it accrues.

Destructive debt: Debt that has higher interest rate costs than the amount of income or wealth generated through the use of borrowed funds.

One last thing to consider in your primary debt management strategy is this: be careful of early repayment penalties. Lenders give you a loan with the expectation of earning enough money from your interest payments to exceed their other outgoings. Sometimes, particularly with big lenders such as those that offer mortgages, the contract guarantees that they will make a minimum amount of money off you and that, if you repay your loan early, the penalties will make up for their lost interest income. This can be a tremendous impediment to an otherwise great debt strategy, but, unfortunately, there isn't much that can be done about it, unless it becomes such a serious issue that you need to start using your options of last resort.

LAST RESORTS

When you simply can't repay your loan as agreed upon in your contract, it may be time to turn to a last resort. You shouldn't even attempt these unless absolutely necessary, because they tend to harm your credit score. Plus, although lenders have the ability to modify your loan terms, they gave you a loan intending that you pay it back with interest; so, they tend to be somewhat rigid unless there is the very real chance that they won't be getting any of the money back.

There is a stigma attached to an inability to pay back your loans—one of being unreliable or irresponsible—but this is a very common situation with any kind of loan, especially variable-rate loans. Recall that variable-rate loans have an interest rate which can change, so you don't always know how much your payments are going to be, particularly with credit cards, the rates of which can more than triple without any reason or notification. This is why my rule of thumb, which you will hear again before you are done reading this book, is this: if you can't do the math to determine the future value of your financial product, then that financial product isn't for you. When it comes to variable-rate loans, these calculations include advanced statistical analytics and econometric analysis, and if you are not familiar with these, then any estimates you have regarding how much you will be paying on your loan in the future are merely a wild guess. Even fixed-rate loans come with the risk of losing your job through economic collapse. More people have run into financial trouble with debt by making uncertain decisions than by making certain but bad decisions. There are a lot of very complicated financial products available, and these exotic loans are generally for a niche market and would not be broadly available to your average consumer, except that the salesperson offering them to you makes money from their sale. None of this is really helpful in hindsight, however, and if you are in a position wherein you cannot repay your loans, it's time to learn from past decisions and put yourself in a position to make better ones.

REMEMBER THIS!!! If you can't do the math to determine the future value of your financial product, then that financial product is not for you.

If you are struggling to pay your debts, don't ignore your lenders or collections agents. Clearly they want your money, and they would rather offer you modified loan terms than get nothing at all. They may offer to lower your monthly payments by extending your repayment period, or they may offer a deferment, wherein you make no payments or reduced payments for several months, but the principal does not change and interest continues to accrue during that time. Sometimes lenders will offer other loan options like consolidation or refinancing, both of which were described earlier in this chapter.

By contrast, if you ignore them, they will continue trying to contact you, which can be stressful, and any late or missed payments will continue to damage your credit rating. In some cases, the lender may even try to take you to court or simply take your possessions. Each country has its own laws regarding the manner in which a lender can treat a borrower, so it wouldn't be possible to include a comprehensive list here, but if you find yourself being unduly harassed by collections agents it may be prudent to use the internet, a lawyer or local credit counsellor to learn your rights as a borrower.

KEY TERMS

Deferment: A temporary halt of loan repayment obligations.

Bankruptcy: A legally obligated restructuring or forgiveness of debt obligations.

If the lender is unwilling to negotiate with you, then it may be time to consider bankruptcy. Bankruptcy means that you go through the legal system to either force your lenders to renegotiate loan terms or to default on your debt (which means that it has been officially recognized as uncollectable and that you are no longer accountable for that debt). Filing for bankruptcy does harm your credit rating, but remember that bankruptcy is a one-time event from which you will slowly recover; if you simply stop making payments, then those debts will continue to harm your credit rating indefinitely until you do something about them.

If your lender decides they want to get their money back no matter what, they may try to take your possessions. For example, when you get a mortgage, the lender puts a lien on your house, which means that if you fail to repay your mortgage, the lender gets ownership of that house—they can, and will, kick you out of your house and resell the property. Lenders may also try to take you to court in order to be given the right to take anything of value to auction up to the amount you owe. In such a case, you may have no other option but to let them take your stuff; sometimes it's actually financially the better option to allow this to happen. This was a particularly common strategy after the 2008 financial collapse, when housing prices plummeted.

For a lot of people, this meant that they owed far more money on their mortgage than the home was actually worth, and some people decided to abandon their homes—they just left and stopped paying their mortgage. If you find yourself in a position in which your mortgage is much higher than the value of your home (known colloquially as 'being underwater'), and you have alternate options for shelter, then it may be prudent to default, let the lender take the house and buy a different one at a much lower price. It's a bold and sometimes risky choice, but it does happen as a method of last resort.

BUILDING (OR REBUILDING) CREDIT

Your credit rating is an objective evaluation of your personal credit risk. (Credit risk is discussed in more detail in chapter 7.) Credit agencies use predetermined, quantitative criteria to estimate the likelihood that you will default on a loan, which is then used by lenders to decide whether they should approve your application and what interest rate they should charge. Globally, the most common credit rating used is your FICO score. FICO (Fair Isaac Corporation) is a private US company that offers analytics products and services to large companies; it is the most commonly cited source for credit information. The criteria FICO uses to calculate your credit score are weighted, with some given more importance than others:

- Payment history: 35 per cent
- Amounts owed: 30 per cent
- Length of credit history: 15 per cent
- New credit: 10 per cent
- Types of credit: 10 per cent

Since your credit rating determines the availability and rates of loans accessible to you, it is a direct determinant of the financial opportunities that await you. Of course a good credit rating will save you lots of money on your debts as you pay less in interest payments, but if you are using debt to fund your investments, then your credit rating also determines whether an investment will make more money than the cost of funding it. Oh, and by the way, lots of employers also look at your credit score to determine whether you are a viable job candidate, so keep that in mind, too.

It's unfortunate that initially building credit, or rebuilding credit after a bankruptcy, is somewhat circular—you need a good credit rating in order to apply for debt, but you can't get a good credit rating until you have been approved for debt. There are a variety of options available for those people in need of an improved credit rating, but be very careful, because there are just as many scams available which seem legitimate. These cons typically either try to charge you for worthless services, trick you into contracts or new debts with terrible terms, or even directly steal your money. Always use due diligence:

- Research an organization before working with them to ensure they are both legitimate and reputable.
- Always read the terms of your agreements before signing.
- Do the calculations to ensure you are being told the truth.
- Never let someone talk you into making a decision that isn't in your own best interest.

A common place to begin building or rebuilding credit is with low-risk debt. This includes things like secured loans, which are debt issued to you but only after you offer something to the lender as collateral. Low-limit credit cards are common as a first form of debt, allowing you to establish a line of credit but only of very little value so that any default will not result in much loss on the part of the lender. If low-limit cards aren't an option, then prepaid credit cards are a sort-of secured loan, in that you must pay for the credit card prior to its use, rather than after use, putting a limit equal to the amount you have prepaid and allowing the lender to incur little or no risk. Contract plans, such as for mobile phones, also help to build your credit rating so long as you make payments on time, and can sometimes be easier to acquire than actual loans, since you are purchasing a service rather than simply being given money.

If you have tried all these options to no avail, then it may be necessary to get a co-signer on your loan. A co-signer is anyone who is willing to guarantee that you will repay your debts and who will be accountable for their repayment if you don't pay them, such as parents who co-sign when their children are first establishing credit. Ideally, your co-signer should have a better credit rating than you do, otherwise it's not much help. Being a co-signer on someone else's loans is extremely risky, though, because the co-signer takes on the risk that the loan applicant will default and puts it on himself rather than on the lender. Late or missing payments, or defaulting, will harm the co-signer as much as the borrower. Particularly for people coming out of bankruptcy, this makes conversations about co-signing extremely difficult, since few really want to co-sign but may do so out of a sense of obligation.

It is very important that you don't apply for too many loans. Most of the major lending institutions have very similar criteria and practices, so if you get rejected for a particular type of loan from one lender, you will most likely get rejected for similar loans by other lenders, too. Applications for new debt affect your credit rating, so perseverance can actually be a hindrance to success. Also, having too many lines of credit can appear suspicious, as can having loan limits that are a very high percentage of your income. In these cases, it may appear to the lenders as though you intend to default in the future after abusing your available debt, or that the amount of debt you have available puts you at high risk of unintentional default given your current annual income. They will reject your application. When one lender sees you have already been rejected by another lender, they are more likely to reject you too, so be aware of what each lender expects and the types of loans they offer before you even apply.

Once you have already been approved for debt, improving your credit score is mostly a matter of common sense. Ensure that you maintain consistent payments, making all your payments on time. Many lenders offer auto-pay features, which automatically withdraw money from your bank account at the same time each month, reducing the chance for missed or late payments. If you use this feature, make sure to keep reviewing your statements anyway, to watch for billing errors. Particularly with credit, it's best to use your credit cards only a little bit each month, and then repay it in full each time. Not only will this help improve your credit rating, but it will ensure that you don't overpay for your purchases. Remember that any money you pay in interest represents an overpayment for the goods you have bought. If possible, maintain a consistent income and keep at least one bank account open with money in it, because the appearance of whether you will be able to repay your loans is a major determinant in your credit worthiness. Try to diversify the types of debt you have—mortgage, car loan, credit card, etc.—maintaining a small balance on each, and do not apply for multiples of each type, but try to have just a little of each type of debt. If you are an independent contractor, entrepreneur or business owner, then protect your credit rating by registering your businesses as limited liability companies. Each country has its own laws about this, but the idea is that it keeps your business finances separate from your personal finances, so that if your business runs into financial trouble it won't harm you personally.

– 6 –

INVESTING

The act of investing includes any expenditure you make which has the sole purpose of generating more value than you originally spent. This is distinct from spending, because mere spending loses value as the items of purchase are either consumed or devalue over time, and it's distinct from gambling, because the potential gains from gambling are based purely on probability rather than on any objective assessment of the intrinsic or potential future value of the expenditure. Investing is notorious for being the most difficult and complicated part of personal financial management, but that doesn't have to be the case. There are a variety of different types of investment and different approaches to investing strategy; some are appropriate only for investment professionals with access to high-end trading technology, while others are completely appropriate for the layperson who just wants to save for their retirement. In this chapter we will take a look at the different ways investments can be made, some of the common types of investments which are available to you, and how you can manage your investment portfolio.

INVESTING INSTITUTIONS

Several different types of organizations make investments available to the public, many offering their services exclusively to companies or functioning as intermediaries. It is extremely common for there to be overlap between *depository* institutions and *investing* institutions, as many full-service financial institutions will offer both to their customers. This can cause confusion as to where to go to get information. Here are the major types of organization which have a direct role in your investing activities.

Broker-dealers

Broker-dealers are the organizations or individuals who facilitate exchanges. They will buy from or sell to you directly through their own investment portfolio, or will function as an intermediary. It used to be that all broker-dealers were individuals who received commission on successful orders, but increasingly there are self-service broker-dealer online platforms that allow you to manage your own transactions at a much lower price.

Exchanges and commercial banks

Both exchanges and commercial banks are organizations you won't deal with directly, unless you work in the field of finance, but they play a critical role. Exchanges are the places where broker-dealers congregate to make trades and corporations make their stocks available to buyers.

Commercial banks are exclusively available to businesses and offer the services necessary for a company to sell stocks, bonds or other financial products (see p. 32). They also offer more typical services to companies, such as providing accounts and issuing loans.

Underwriters

You may be familiar with insurance underwriters, which assess how likely you are to file a claim (i.e., how risky you are to the insurance company). Banking and securities underwriters can be found in commercial banks or as dedicated companies and assess the risk of a company or person borrowing money. For investors, this is most frequently expressed in terms of a 'grade on bonds'. If you are buying a bond (a form of debt discussed later in this chapter), you will want to know how likely the bond issuer is to fail in their bond repayments. This is published as a letter grade system unique to each underwriter. Securities underwriters inspect a company's finances to ensure that everything is within regulation and to determine its value, the number of shares of stock to issue and the amount of money the company is likely to raise selling stocks. They also help with the sale through something called an 'initial public offering' (IPO). The IPO is where the corporation raises funds by selling ownership of its company; nearly all the trading that happens after that is between investors, called the 'secondary market'. A single corporation can have more than one IPO if they are creating and selling new shares of stock, but a single share of stock can have only one IPO. If a company wants to rebuy their own stock, it's called 'treasury stock', which can then be resold on the secondary market.

Funds

Funds are pools of investments managed by a professional investor. Lots of people give their money to the fund, it is invested for them, and each person earns a rate of returns consistent with the overall changes in value to the fund. It is as though you have purchased a variety of investments, except you have actually only purchased a share in one fund, which is composed of a variety of investments. There are two types of funds: passive and active. They both have the same basic structure and functionality but the management style between them differs.

Passive funds start with a single investment portfolio and simply leave it alone, changing it only when deemed absolutely necessary. For example, index funds maintain a portfolio of investments consistent with a single stock index. This may seem negligent at first, but index funds consistently and continuously outperform active funds.

Active funds include hedge funds and most mutual funds. Active funds require the attention of full-time investors, and thus carry higher fees and costs than passive funds. A hedge fund pools the assets of its investors to collectively invest their money using strategies which are fluid and can change as the hedge fund manager decides. By contrast, mutual funds maintain an investment portfolio whose strategy must strictly adhere to that described when the fund is formed, and they sell shares like stock. Sometimes this means creating and selling a fixed number of shares (as with normal stock), known as a 'closed-end mutual fund'. Other times this means creating or eliminating as many shares as necessary as people buy and sell their stake in the mutual fund, known as an 'open-end mutual fund'. The other main difference between hedge and mutual funds is their fee structure: hedge funds tend to charge according to the performance of the fund, while the fees charged by a mutual fund are strictly regulated.

Wealth management firms

Be very wary of the individuals at these organizations. While there are legitimate advisors who can assist you with managing your finances, the wealth management industry is also filled with frauds. The problem is that this isn't a finance job so much as a sales position. To find a reliable advisor:

- Check for credentials, such as certifications, degrees or charter memberships.
- Check their portfolio to see if they have had success in the past.
- Interview other clients or check for testimonials. (Confiden-

tiality may make this difficult, but find a reference from someone you trust.)

- Check their employment history to see if there is anything that supports their credentials, or appears to be sketchy.
- Check public records for any criminal or civil suits against them.
- Check their credit history to see if they successfully manage their own finances.
- Talk to them to see if they appear knowledgeable and trustworthy. Don't feel obligated—if you don't feel comfortable, just keep looking.

CAPITAL MANAGEMENT

There is a very simple equation in finance which describes your approach to capital management: Assets = Debt + Equity. In other words, everything you own was funded either by incurring debt or by expending your own resources. Clearly, the money and things you own are an asset to you, but people tend to forget that debt is an asset, too, since debt is used to fund the purchase of assets. If you play with this, subtracting all your debt from the total value of your assets shows you how much equity (net wealth) you have accumulated. The balance of debt and equity you have used to fund the value of your assets is a critical portion of your financial management strategy, known as 'capital management'.

TRY IT NOW! Start with the current value of your home, then subtract the remaining balance of your mortgage, and that's the amount of equity you have in your home. This isn't just an abstract value, as you can actually borrow money using the equity in your home as collateral.

Whether you use debt or equity to fund your asset ownership, there are costs of debt and equity involved, known collectively as the 'cost of capital'. The cost of debt refers to the amount of interest you will pay over the life of your debt (see chapters 3 and 5). Most people don't realize that there is also a cost associated with using your own resources to purchase assets, known as the 'cost of equity'. 'Opportunity cost' is the value of the next best option; so if you have the choice between purchasing furniture and keeping your money in a bank account, the opportunity cost of buying the furniture is equal to the amount of interest you would have earned by keeping your money in the account. This makes most purchases far more expensive than people realize, since each purchase you make not only includes spending money, but also losing any earnings on that money if you hadn't spent it.

Effective capital management requires you to assess the cheapest sources of both debt and equity being used to fund your assets, and also to find the proper balance of equity and debt so that you choose the cheaper of the two at any given point. As you come to rely on one more than the other, its costs will start to increase; the more debt you have, the more lenders will start to charge you in interest rates as a result of the shift in your credit report. If you rely more on equity, you will begin to pull assets which are more valuable, making debt cheaper compared to the money you would be losing by selling your investments. The goal is to maintain the lowest cost of capital possible, using variations on the core equation:

$$\text{Cost of capital} = ((E/A)^{*}CE) + ((D/A)^{*}CD)$$

Don't panic yet! It's simpler than it looks.

Step 1: Replace the letters with the following values:

E = the amount of equity you have

D = the amount of debt you have

A = the total value of your assets

CE = the average cost of your equity (the money you would earn on the next best option)

CD = the average cost of your debt (the interest payments you will make)

Step 2: Divide *E* by *A*, and then divide *D* by *A*. This 'weights' each source of capital so that the percentage of your assets funded by each equity and debt is represented, rather than just assuming it's 50/50.

Step 3: Multiply each by their respective average cost, then stop here for a moment. This part alone is important in that it helps you to assess whether your debt or equity is costing you more money, helping you to determine the proper balance. If these aren't about equal, it's likely you could fund your assets more cheaply.

Step 4: Add them together. This is your total cost of capital. The question remaining is whether your assets, on average, are generating more value than they are costing. If yes, good for you. If not, keep trying, because right now you are losing money on your assets. This equation gives you only a rough idea of your cost of capital, though. The more precise you can be, even to the point of breaking down each source of debt and equity individually, the more accurate your calculation will be.

PERSONAL BALANCE SHEET

The best method to keep track of the value of your assets, and by extension your accumulated wealth, is to create a personal balance sheet, which tracks the details of your balance of Assets = Debt + Equity.

Assets	**$X**	**Debt**	**$X**
Item 1	$X	Item 1	$X
Item 2	$X	Item 2	$X
Item 3	$X	**Equity**	**$X**
Item 4	$X	Item 1	$X
Item 5	$X	Item 2	$X

Your personal balance sheet should have a structure similar to this example. In the left column, list each of your assets, including their value at the end of the period. Note that assets such as your car will decrease in value over time (a process called depreciation), while other assets such as your home may increase in value over time (a process called appreciation), so account for these changes, rather than listing the value at purchase. In the right column, list each of your debts and their ending value for the period, as well as your equity. For example, if your only asset is a house worth $100,000, your personal balance sheet may look like this:

Assets	**$100,000**	**Debt**	**$80,000**
House	$100,000	Mortgage	$80,000
		Equity	**$20,000**
		Home equity	$20,000

You can use your personal balance sheet to assess how much value you have, what contributes to your value, and how your capital is being managed. You can also assess your wealth management; changes in the value of the different items over time will indicate whether you are gaining or losing value. Assuming that you plan to retire (see chapter 9), your balance sheet should show a gradual increase in the value of your assets, as well as a gradual reduction in debt, associated with a gradual increase in equity. Still, if your cost of capital is too high, causing you to lose money, it may be prudent to reduce your total assets in order to reduce those costs and put yourself in a position of earning value again. For example, it's not uncommon for people who get their first permanent job or who otherwise acquire their first large amount of money (such as an inheritance or a signing bonus) to spend their money on an expensive car, only to realize that the cost of fuel, insurance and maintenance means they will lose money slowly over time. Selling the car will reduce their total assets, but also their cost of capital, allowing them to slowly regain that value in a sustainable manner.

COMMON TYPES OF INVESTMENTS

The saying goes: 'Bulls make money, bears make money and hogs get slaughtered.' Being 'bullish' means that you believe values will increase; being 'bearish' means that you believe values will decrease; being a hog means that you are sitting on your finances and not paying attention. Whether the markets increase or decrease in value, there are a variety of investment types, which present opportunities to benefit.

Bonds

Bonds are a form of debt in which you can invest. When an organization wants to borrow money, it can issue bonds, the price of which goes to the organization under contract agreement to repay the money to the investor with interest. Once the bond is purchased, it can be resold again and again until the date of final repayment (known as the 'date of maturity'), and the organization which issued the bonds will then repay the debt to whoever owns the bond. Bonds tend to be a little safer than some investments because they get priority over equity investors in getting their money back if the issuer fails and liquidates their assets, but there is still the risk of default. Part of what intimidates people about bonds is all the new terminology associated with them. Here are the key concepts:

- **Ask**: The price at which investors are willing to sell a bond; this term is used in relation to most financial exchanges.
- **Bid**: The price at which investors are willing to buy a bond; this term is used in relation to most financial exchanges.
- **Spread**: The difference between the ask and bid prices. The sale of bonds only occurs when an investor is willing to increase their bid or decrease their ask to a value attractive to other investors.
- **Face value/Par value**: The amount of money that will be given to the bond holder on maturity of the bond
- **Maturity**: The date at which a bond will be repaid by the issuer
- **Rate/Discount**: Bonds are sold at a price lower than the face value in an amount equivalent to the amount of interest the bond will earn upon maturity; they are said to be sold at a

'discount' of their face value, which means you are getting something of greater value at a discounted rate, which accounts for the interest rate you will earn.

- **Issuer:** The organization which initially sells the bond, and who will repay its value
- **Price:** The price for which bonds are selling
- **Price change:** The amount of change in a bond's price over the previous period
- **Yield:** The rate of returns a person will experience by purchasing a bond at a particular price in a given year
- **Yield change:** The amount of change in a bond's yield over the previous period
- **Yield to maturity (YTM):** The rate of returns a person will experience if the bond, and all coupons, are held until the maturity date
- **Volume:** The number of bonds bought or sold during a given period
- **Credit quality:** The amount of risk that an issuer has of defaulting, as assessed by underwriters
- **Corporate bonds:** Bonds issued by corporations—they vary widely in rate and risk
- **Government bonds:** Bonds issued by governments can range widely in time to maturity, but short-term government debt lasting 30 days or fewer is considered a risk-free rate, since government debt tends to be safer than other types. Some have tax exemptions, depending on the country.

- **Convertible bonds:** A special type of corporate bond (issued by a corporation) which gives you the option to exchange the bond for a given number of shares of stock—a great option if a company's stock price rises drastically during the time before maturity

- **Callable bonds:** A special type of bond which gives the issuer the option to recall their bonds by paying the current value plus a penalty to the issuer, should interest rates drop enough that the penalties are less than the amount saved by issuing bonds at the lower interest rates

- **Puttable bonds:** A special type of bond which gives the investor the option to force the issuer to repay the value of the bond minus a penalty. These are good for investors when interest rates increase dramatically, so that they can get their money back and reinvest it in higher-rate bonds, assuming that the increased earning potential is greater than the penalty they will pay.

- **Registered vs. Bearer bonds:** A long time ago, all bonds were bearer bonds, which meant that whoever was in physical possession of the bond was the owner. Thanks to better record keeping and technology, now nearly all bonds are 'registered' to the owner by a serial number.

- **Coupon bonds:** Whereas typical bonds pay their total value upon maturity, coupon bonds make several payments ('coupons') over the course of their life, maturity simply being the final payment.

- **Junk bonds:** Issued by issuers with a very high risk of default. The higher risk means they have to offer higher interest rates to attract investors. While junk bonds do have legitimate use for investors, they became notorious as less than savoury financial advisors sold them to unsuspecting elderly people who were accustomed to the safety of government bonds, resulting in a lot of lost wealth.

Bond: An investment in the debt of an organization.

Capital

A scarce few hard assets that you will have the option to purchase can be considered investments—only those things you buy with the intent of earning more money than you paid. If you purchase real estate with the intention of charging rent or accruing equity, or if you invest in a machine that produces goods which can be sold as a part of your business, it's considered a capital investment. Capital investments are common for venture capitalists, entrepreneurs, business owners and the self-employed. They are made by innovative people who find ways to turn the things they own into income or who invest in collector items, such as wine, art or classic cars—things which will not provide income, but which the investor hopes will increase in value for the purpose of being resold at a later date. These markets can be very fickle, though, and are recommended only for those already extremely familiar with the relevant market, who are willing to take a high degree of risk. Since collector items are unique, they cannot be easily traded, and must generally be sold at an auction or through a dealer.

Stocks

Stocks are a share of ownership in a corporation. The people who run a corporation aren't necessarily its owners—the owners are the stockholders. When a company wants to raise money, the company is split into a number of equivalent pieces, and each piece is sold to investors. As the company increases in value, so do the shares of stock. Additionally, all the profits a company earns belong to the stockholders. The corporation can choose to keep the money as 'retained earnings', which are reinvested into the corporation's growth, but if the corporation can't or won't use that money to fund growth, it must be distributed among the stockholders in the form of 'dividends'. Stockholders also get rights related to corporate decisions, but the exact nature depends on the type of stock.

The value of stocks tends to be extremely volatile in the short term, fluctuating with investor sentiment, behavioural trends (discussed in chapter 10) and the portfolio strategies of major institutional investors like broker-dealers and hedge funds. Over the long term (usually weeks or months, though particularly large bubbles of overvaluation can take years to correct), a corporation's stock price tends to float around the intrinsic value of its assets plus an adjustment to account for future earnings potential. These are the key concepts associated with stocks:

- **Common stock:** Allows you to vote on the board of directors and on certain corporate decisions, and gives you rights to corporate financial information and any profits not used as retained earnings or to pay the dividends of preferred stockholders, in a split equal to the number of shares outstanding (the total number of shares of stock which are owned)

- **Preferred stock:** A lot like common stock, except that it doesn't give you voting rights, but it does give you guaranteed dividends

- **Asset-backed securities (ABS):** Ownership of specific investments or operations, rather than ownership in a company. The most common type is the *mortgage-backed security (MBS)*, in which a bank raises money by selling shares of MBS to mortgage borrowers to buy homes, who then repay their principal, the interest or both to the investor. They became notorious during the 2008 financial collapse, when several major banks passed off high-risk MBS to unsuspecting investors without telling them they included a high proportion of subprime loans (loans to people who are at high risk of default).

- **Buying or selling long**: A standard transaction, wherein any changes in value are directly and instantly yours to incur. Buy long when you think the price will go up; sell long when you think the price will go down.
- **Selling short**: You borrow a stock and sell it to someone else with a promise to repurchase it at a later date. This is done when you think a stock will go down in price, allowing you to sell it at the current market price and repurchase it at a lower price, then to sell it long or keep it with the expectation that the price will recover. Selling short is extremely risky because if a stock continues to increase in value, you could end up having to rebuy it at a price much higher than what you sold it for.
- **Buying on margin**: Buying stock using borrowed money. You must eventually repay that money with interest, so this is only effective if your stock earnings are higher than your interest rate.
- **Market orders**: Orders that occur at current market price
- **Stop and Limit orders**: Triggered when a stock reaches a particular price. A stop order sells a stock when its price drops below a given price to limit potential losses, or buys a stock

when it reaches that low price if the investor believes the price will go back up. A limit order buys a stock when its price rises to a given price at which the investor feels that the stock will continue to maintain stable growth, or sells it at that high price if the investor believes the price will drop again after reaching a peak.

- **Time contingent orders**: Orders that are put on a time delay or cancelled after a given amount of time
- **Pegged orders**: Orders that do not execute until some trigger other than the stock's price is observed, such as a change in value of a stock index or in some economic metric like employment
- **Blue chip stocks**: Issued by large, global corporations. They have limited growth potential but tend to be very stable during market shocks.
- **Green chip stocks**: Issued by companies that work in environmental sustainability industries, such as green energy
- **Red chip stocks**: Issued by Chinese companies in a market outside China
- **Cap**: Refers to the size of a company's market capitalization (the collective value of their stocks), from large caps (>$10 billion) to nano caps (<$50 million)
- **Penny stocks**: Extremely cheap stocks, with a price of less than $0.01, which must often be bought and sold in blocks. They belong to very small firms in industries conducting uncertain research or creating experimental products, or in new industries. They sometimes can indicate fraudulent operations.

Derivatives

Derivatives tend to scare people due to the way that they are misused by professional investors. They were originally developed as a way to mitigate risk, but once people discovered that they could be used to generate extremely high-risk income (and even to hide corporate losses from investors in a fraud that can be very difficult to detect), they gained notoriety as the representation of everything crooked in the financial sector. Derivatives are actually just contracts to participate in some future transaction. In other words, the value of the contract is derived from the assets named in the contract, giving them the name 'derivative'. Each type of derivative is unique and can be used to limit risk as well as to generate income.

KEY TERM **Derivatives**: Contracts for the exchange of investments that are bought and sold prior to the actual exchange.

Forwards and futures

The very first derivatives contracts were 'forwards', which were developed as a way to stabilize the price and availability of agricultural products. Traditionally, crop prices would be very high and availability very low during the off season, but shortly after harvest the markets were overflowing with goods. Farmers never knew exactly how much to bring and sometimes even left the food they couldn't sell rotting rather than incur the expense of shipping it back; they received terrible profits, since the flood of competition drove prices down for each crop when it was in season. To facilitate increased certainty in production and price, forward contracts were developed: an agreement for someone to purchase a given quantity of a specific crop, at a predetermined price, on a specific date. Forwards are flexible and can be customized, so long as both buyer and seller agree, but this flexibility means that they are difficult to resell.

That's why futures were developed. Futures are like forwards, except they are standardized contracts for common goods, always for the same volume, in blocks that mature on the same date, sold for the same price and with the same contractual terms. This allows futures to be traded like stocks, which many investors do as a way to generate income.

Forward: A customizable contract that guarantees the terms of exchange at a future date.

Future: A standardized contract that guarantees the terms of exchange at a future date, which can be traded like equities.

Options

Since forwards and futures are contractual obligations to participate in an exchange at a given price, if the market price is significantly different, it can create potential for significant gain or loss. For example, it's rather unfortunate if you have a contract to buy 100 kilograms of corn at $100 each (these prices are not representative of reality) and the market price of corn drops to $10 per kilogram. This is why options contracts are so popular—they do not obligate you to participate in the exchange, but give you the option to do so on or before a given date.

There are two types of options. Buying a 'call option' gives you the choice to purchase a given volume of something at a specified price, so long as you do so before the maturity date. Buying a 'put option' gives you the choice to sell a given volume of something at a specified price. Regardless of what happens to the market price, the seller of the option is obligated to participate in the exchange if the buyer decides to exercise the option ('exercise' meaning the buyer chooses to participate in the contractual exchange). As a buyer, if the market price does not move in your favour, then you successfully ward off risk by exercising the option. If the market price does move in your favour you can simply allow the option to expire and participate in the exchange at the market rate.

KEY TERM **Option**: A contract that gives the purchaser the right, and the seller the obligation, to participate in an exchange at established terms should the purchaser choose to exercise their right.

There can be some pretty severe risk involved with options. From the seller's perspective, selling options represents an opportunity to generate income, but it also represents risks, putting them in a position for serious loss if any major movement occurs in the market price. Second, when companies sell options and then the market changes in a way that benefits the buyer, the company can have lost a significant amount of money that won't appear on any of their financial statements until the buyer exercises their options, making these losses invisible and creating the potential for fraudulent misuse to artificially inflate the value of the company, thereby driving up the stock price for the personal gain of the executives.

Private investors can buy and sell options, too, which is particularly common for stocks. When including stock options as a part of your investment portfolio, a number of strategies present themselves.

BEGINNER STRATEGIES FOR INVESTMENT

Investing strategies aren't just about picking the best investments you can find, but about picking investments that are more beneficial together than they are on their own. Now that you know a thing or two about the various investments available to you, you are able to build some basic strategies.

The most common strategy is simple diversification of investments. For bonds, this means staggering your coupon and maturity dates not only to provide consistent income, but also so that you can more readily respond to changes in the market, rather than having the entirety of your bond investments tied up at the same time. For stocks, this means picking high-quality investments which tend to fluctuate in price in opposite directions; as one stock decreases in value in the short run, another should increase, but both should appreciate over the long run. In the same manner, including global diversification of stock investments can reduce the impact of global trends. For example, after the 2008 financial collapse, Western stocks plummeted, while many Eastern stocks slowed their growth but maintained stability. Also, diversifying the types of investments you have can help you find an appropriate balance of potential gain and risk—maintaining a percentage of your portfolio in stocks, or even high-risk investments like speculative stocks or junk bonds, and the remainder of your portfolio in low-risk investments.

KEY TERM **Diversification**: The act of investing in several different investments to reduce the potential value of loss if a single investment fails.

Many options make use of a combination of stocks and derivatives. For example, buying stocks as well as a put option gives you the upside potential of the stock but limits your potential losses by guaranteeing you will be able to resell the stock at the price noted in the option. So long as your gains exceed the purchase cost of the put option, you will remain 'in the black'. Similarly, if you believe a stock will decrease in price, you can sell it short and then buy a call option, so that if you are wrong you can repurchase the stock at a guaranteed maximum price, putting a limit on the immense risk associated with shorting stock.

Some investing strategies utilize more than one option. For example, buying both a call and a put option with the same strike price (the price at which you can exercise your option) means that you will make money regardless of which direction the stock moves, so long as the move is large enough that you earn more money than the cost of the options. This strategy is known as a 'straddle'. In a strategy known as the 'collar', you buy a stock and sell a call option on the stock, so that if the price of the stock increases, the option buyer will likely exercise their option; this creates limited upside potential, but the money from the sale of the call option can be used to fund a put option, so that you eliminate the cost of the option. The result is that you create both a 'floor' and a 'cap' (a maximum amount of loss and gain, respectively), functioning as a collar that limits the amount of movement in the stock price.

The strategies available to you are varied and numerous. As you get more practice using them, you can expand to develop multi-step strategies in which the outcome of one strategy will trigger additional strategic transactions.

VALUATION METHODS

Even the best investing strategies won't help you if you don't understand the value of the investments you are making. Without assessing the future potential of your investments, you are simply gambling by letting probability take over. It is in the nature of investment valuation that the calculations of their value are mathematical, but when you take them step-by-step, they are really quite simple.

The end result of how much money you make (or lose) on an investment is called the 'return on investment' (ROI). In calculating ROI, we are concerned with the percentage of increase or decrease in value over your initial investment, not the actual monetary value you have earned or lost. The simple calculation is:

$$\text{ROI} = (P - C)/C$$

P is the current market price at which you sold the investment, and C is the cost of the investment—the price you paid for it. So, if you had $100 to invest ($C$) and your investment increased in value to $110 ($P$), your ROI is 10 per cent.

Another common valuation method, typically used with fixed-income investments such as bonds and bank accounts, is future value (see chapter 3). Calculating the future value allows you to determine how much money an investment made today will be worth at any time in the future, assuming a fixed rate of return. In other words, if you put $100 in a fixed-rate investment today and want to know what it will be worth in ten years, you would calculate future value.

Present value (PV) is the complete opposite. It starts with a known end value for an investment—such as with bonds for which you will receive the face value of the bond—and then determines how much it's worth right now. It's commonly used in capital asset investments, to determine whether the operations of those investments are keeping up with estimates of its total productive value. The calculation for present value is:

$$\text{PV} = P/(1 + r)^t$$

P is the amount of money you will receive at the end of the investment's life, r is the rate of return you are earning on the investment during that time, and t is the amount of time that passes (in years) between now and the end of the investment's life. For example, a known future value of $100, which will earn 1 per cent per year for ten years, is worth $90.53 today. $90.53 = $100/(1 + 0.01)^{10}. This is an extremely common calculation with bonds, since bonds are sold at the discounted rate (the present value), and you must estimate whether the market price of the bond is above or below the present value to determine whether the price is worth it.

While present value is fine for simple bonds, coupon bonds pay several times, as do a variety of other investments discussed in this chapter. To determine the present value of such an investment, or for your portfolio of many investments (assuming they are all fixed-rate), you can use net present value (NPV). When calculating NPV, calculate the present values of each payment you will receive, and then add them together. If you have several payments of $100 over the next few years, then assuming they all have the same rate of return, each payment will have a smaller PV as the date extends further away from the current date. The reason for this is that more time must pass before you get that payment, so while interest is collecting over the greater period of time, the value at present will be smaller. Imagine that your investment, at 1 per cent interest, will earn $100 in ten years and another $100 in twenty years (making two payments, with a total future value of $200); we would add together the PV of each to get an NPV of $172.48. You would add your earlier PV calculation to the second payment's calculation of $100/(1 + 0.01)^{20} = $81.95.

Present value: The value that an investment with known future value has at the present time.

Net present value (NPV): The sum of present values on an investment that generates multiple cash flows.

Absolute and relative models

The value of fixed-rate investments is easy because you have certainty regarding what you will earn. The problems come when you start estimating the value of variable-rate investments, like stocks or derivatives. There are many complicated methods of calculating variable-rate investments, but they fall into three categories: absolute, relative and hybrid models.

Absolute models are the most popular among investors who look for the *intrinsic value* of an investment, rather than attempting to benefit by trading on movements in the market. Such models include calculations of the liquidation value of the company, often adjusted for growth over the next few years. In other words, you start with what the company would be worth if you simply sold everything it has for the cash, then subtract their debt. Of course, the value of companies changes over time, and the market price of stocks is often based on the future earning potential of the company, rather than its current earnings. So, estimates of liquidation value start with the current liquidation value, and then increase that value by a percentage consistent with their average past growth, or by some other estimate of their future growth rate. Not every share of a single company's stock is going to be worth the value of the entire company, so you must divide the liquidation value by the number of shares of stock outstanding, to calculate the *liquidation value per share*.

For investors who prefer investments that yield *dividends*, the dividend discount model (DDM) is popular. DDM is calculated by working out the NPV of future dividends. If you estimate that dividends will grow over that period, simply subtract the growth rate from the rate of return in the NPV calculation. For dividend investors, if the NPV of the dividends is lower than the current market price per share of stock, the stock is undervalued, making it a great deal.

Relative models are popular among traders, who invest based on short-term movements in the market, because they allow them to compare the performance of various options. For example, it's common to compare the performance of an investment against index funds to determine which has a higher rate of returns each period, or to compare the rates of return of competing companies within a single sector or against the economic growth rate of the company's home country.

Common tools used in performing these comparative assessments use the financial statements of a company and include:

- **Price to earnings ratio (P/E) = Market price per share/ Earnings per share.** This functions as an indicator of the price you are paying for the profits a company will earn for you, either as dividends or through the investment of retained earnings.
- **Return on equity (ROE) = Net income/Shareholder equity.** This indicates the amount of money a company makes using the money shareholders have invested in the company.
- **Operating margin = Operating income/Net sales.** This indicates how efficiently a company is operating.

Each of these indicators is merely that. They are not calculations of company value, but indicators of the comparative performance of companies in which one might invest. Often a combination of indicators is used, included in a single mathematical formula. Other times absolute and relative models are combined to create hybrids that attempt to estimate the value of a stock by combining the intrinsic value of the company with how well it performs compared to other potential investments.

– 7 –

RISK MANAGEMENT

In finance, risk is considered a type of cost. Specifically, risk refers to the likelihood that your assets will decrease in value. This may sound like depreciation—the process by which an asset you own decreases in value over time over the course of its usable lifespan—but risk is unique in that it applies to the probability of losses occurring, and the potential value of those losses. All the decisions you make have some degree of inherent risk. Inaction too often has the greatest amount of risk, so rather than becoming paralyzed by attempting to avoid all risk, look at it as a type of cost that allows you to calculate whether a financial decision will reap greater benefits than the potential losses and to compare the available options. There are a variety of different ways to avoid risk, reduce risk, or even share risk, but each of these has a price. By calculating the cost-value of specific risks, it becomes possible to determine whether any of the tools available for managing risk are financially viable and are themselves an appropriate risk. Risk management is a critical part of financial success, so in this chapter we are going to explore the different types of financial risk, the ways in which risk is measured, and how to effectively manage the amount of risk to which you are exposed.

SPECIFIC RISK

There are several types of risk that can cause you financial losses, most of which are categorized broadly as 'specific risks', which are the risks unique to an individual person or company. In other words, specific risks impact each person and organization uniquely, depending on the nature of their operations and financial management.

Risk: The probability and value of financial loss.

Specific risk: Risk that is associated with an individual investment.

Operating risk

Operating risk includes any of one's primary operations that could cause a financial loss. For many people who work in treacherous careers, such as the military or construction, injury is a real professional risk—one that will not only seriously impact a person's future earning potential, but which will also increase the person's costs as they adapt to their new limitations. Companies with high operating risks can make investors nervous.

In relation to the individual, operating risk includes the operations of sustaining your life. For example, everyone is at risk of losing their income, but how you have managed your assets will affect whether this will be devastating or not. If you have lived modestly and have allocated as much of your money as possible to paying off your mortgage, then losing your job may mean an early retirement rather than a desperate struggle for work and potential homelessness. So, given the choice between refinancing your home (including an almost 100 per cent payment of the remaining principal to avoid the early repayment penalties on a high-principal mortgage) or allocating your money to equity investments, the decision you make will be one of risk management. In both cases you will be earning long-term returns on investment, but home repayment will greatly mitigate your financial risks, while equity investments will increase your risks.

Interest rate risk

The goal of investment is to generate a positive return, but it's not enough to simply earn more money than you invested. Inflation is the process by which the purchasing power of a currency decreases, meaning that you must pay more for things than you did in the past. Consider that the price of bread is now much higher than it was 50 years ago, but wages have also increased during that time period, so that the price of bread as a percentage of your income has probably not changed, unless you are among the very small percentage of people whose incomes increase at a faster rate than inflation.

This is the nature of interest rate risk. Interest rate risk is generally applied to fixed-income investments that generate interest, such as bonds, bank accounts and money market accounts. However, even variable-income investments such as equities must increase in value at a faster rate than your local inflation rate; otherwise you will lose money and would be better off investing in inflation-pegged bonds.

The amount of money you make, measured in terms of the total amount of currency you receive, is called your nominal income (see p. 115). This refers merely to the *volume* of currency you receive in a given year but says nothing about the *value* of that currency. Inflation, which has several different sources, causes your income to devalue, so you must continue to earn more money each year so that your income will continue to purchase an equal volume of goods and services. If you continue to experience inflation, as all countries do nearly 100 per cent of the time, but your income does not increase by at least an equivalent rate, then your real income will go down. Your real income is the amount of money you make, adjusted for changes in prices caused by inflation. So, if your income increases by 2 per cent next year and inflation is 1 per cent during the same time, then not only has your nominal income increased, but so has your real income. This distinction also applies to investments, as inflation can cause your real ROI to be smaller than your nominal ROI, or can even cause you to lose money on an investment.

Credit risk

When a lender loans money to someone, there's always the risk that the borrower simply won't pay the money back, known as 'credit risk'. Whenever you apply for a loan, the lender will do an evaluation of your credit history to see whether you are a high credit risk. Since risk is seen as a type of cost, if you are considered a high credit risk, then lenders will charge you a higher interest rate in order to account for the increased costs associated with lending you the money. The problem this creates is known as a 'loan paradox'—the elevated costs associated with lending money to someone who is a high credit risk forces the lender to charge higher interest rates, but the higher interest rates increase the borrower's payments, thereby increasing the likelihood that they will not be able to repay the loan. Credit risk applies to all types of debt, including bonds, consumer loans and mortgages, business loans, government debt, and even the period in which one person sells a service and waits for their customer to pay the invoice. Credit risk not only influences whether you will get money owed to you, but the perception that others have of whether you will repay money you owe influences the amount of capital available to you and the terms to which you will need to agree.

Liquidity risk

Owning assets and investments can be great, but it doesn't matter how wealthy you are if everything you own is tied up and completely incapable of meeting your short-term needs. Liquidity refers to how quickly your assets can be turned into cash, the most liquid of assets. Liquid assets include timed bank accounts, debt investments which mature within the next month or money owed to you by your employer. All these things can quickly and easily put tangible currency in your pocket. Some assets are not so easy to turn into cash, however; real estate, antiques, vehicles, machinery, companies and other things which are either rare or have an extremely high market price can be difficult to sell in a short period of time. It's possible to be wealthy and still go bankrupt if you own huge volumes of wealth, but it's all tied up in illiquid assets. Liquidity risk refers to the potential for a person or company to fail to keep enough cash or other liquid assets available to pay for short-term costs. To sell an asset for cash is known as 'liquidation'; having enough cash to pay your bills is known as being 'solvent'; while not having enough cash to pay your bills is known as being 'insolvent'.

Prior to the 2008 financial crisis, banks began offering what were known as 'subprime mortgages', advertising these loans by saying: 'Bad credit? No credit? No problem!' Clearly these borrowers were a very high credit risk, and the loans being offered were often systematically much higher than the borrowers could feasibly repay. So, borrowers would repay their mortgages as best as they could, repaying both principal and interest to lenders and even paying penalties when payments were missed; finally banks would repossess the houses when payments stopped. This process gave banks a huge volume of extremely cheap real estate, since they had paid for the houses, but then received a huge discount in the form of the percentage of the total market price paid by borrowers. What made this particular case unique was that banks had underestimated the amount of short-term losses they would sustain once people began defaulting on their mortgages, and they ran out of money reserves. Much of the global financial sector came to a halt as a result of poor risk management—banks incurred greater amounts of credit risk but did not adjust their liquidity risk by increasing the amount of money held in reserve, as would have been appropriate.

Forex risk

If you have ever worked in another country, received foreign currency from a customer or invested in a foreign company, you have been exposed to forex risk. 'Forex' is an abbreviation of 'foreign exchange' and is used in the context of currency exchange rates. As the exchange rate between two currencies fluctuates, the possibility exists that this will cause a change in the value of your income, assets, contracts and transactions; this possibility is called forex risk. On the other hand, with forex risk, one person's loss is another person's gain, so there is the possibility that you will benefit from these shifts in exchange rate.

THINK ABOUT IT

If you buy something online from a foreign country and before the item arrives the exchange rate changes in a way that would have made the product significantly cheaper, you have spent more than you otherwise would. Alternatively, if you spend some time working abroad, earning foreign currency, and while you are away the exchange rate shifts in such a way that the currency you are earning is worth less than your home currency, then you will return home with less money than you expected when you first left.

A sub-type of forex risk is called 'convertibility risk'. While not common, many countries implement restrictions on the exchange or repatriation of their currency. Some countries completely ban taking currency out of the country, in the belief that forcing people to keep currency within their borders will cause additional spending that will stimulate economic growth. Other countries place lesser prohibitions on exchange, such as in China, where there is an upper limit on the total amount of yuan each person is allowed to exchange per day. In some circumstances, a currency cannot be exchanged simply because nobody wants it, as happened in 2008 in Zimbabwe when the currency lost value at such an immense rate that it lost all functional use. All this can place limitations on your ability to manage your finances.

Off-balance-sheet risk

Off-balance-sheet risk is a risk that is known by corporate executives but not always reported, creating for potential investors the illusion of financial health in a company which can be in serious trouble. Counterintuitively, this type of risk comes from the use of tools originally intended to limit the amount of risk to which investors and companies were exposed. Derivatives (see p. 85) are contracts into which people and companies can enter which obligate one or more parties to buy or sell things at some future date and under guaranteed terms. While there are certainly immense benefits to this when used properly, this creates a circumstance in which a company is guaranteed to lose (spend) a significant amount of money at some future date, which does not yet have any influence on the company's financial statements, causing these statements to report a company value greatly above its actual value. This is one method Enron used to obscure their financial performance, hiding devastating losses that would have otherwise caused share price to plummet.

MARKET RISK

While specific risk refers to the likelihood that an individual person, company or investment will experience a loss of value, market risk refers to the likelihood that the entire economy will suffer, causing everyone to lose financial value even if they are not directly associated with the cause of the problem. During the 2008 financial collapse, for example, even businesses that were well managed and financially stable saw losses.

Market risk is generally the result of economic factors, such as unemployment rates, inflation rates, growth, trade and other matters that impact one or more entire countries. Sociopolitical factors can also be a driving force behind market risk, however, in that changes to the legal environment or social trends can be economically self-destructive.

KEY TERM **Market risk**: Risk of financial loss resulting from overall economic decline.

RISK ANALYSIS

You are probably familiar with an old cliché in finance: 'no risk, no reward', but there is absolutely *no reason* to think that accepting risk inherently generates financial returns. The reality is the opposite: all other things being equal, higher risk causes you lower financial gain, since the costs you incur as a result of the elevated risk corrode the value of your assets. All other things being equal between two distinct investment options, if one option has greater risk, then the organization selling that investment must offer a higher rate of return in order to attract investors. It's not that the higher risk causes higher returns—it's that investors *demand* higher returns in order to accept the higher risk.

This relationship between risk and returns is most simply explained with a very basic model known as the 'capital asset pricing model' (CAPM), which looks like this:

$$r_s = r_f + \text{ß}(r_m - r_f)$$

Don't worry, it's not as scary as it looks. All it says is that for an investor to be interested in a specific investment, the returns on that specific investment (r_s) must be higher than the risk-free rate (r_f), at least in an amount great enough to validate the extra risk (ß). CAPM really is as simple as that, but, unfortunately, its assessment of risk is completely wrong, so CAPM is really only functional for educational purposes. CAPM uses an erroneous measure of risk, ß, which is beta. Beta is not a measure of risk, it's a measure of *volatility*, which compares movements in the market price of a single investment to movements in the investment market as a whole. The latter is usually assessed using indices, such as stock indices (e.g., FTSE 100) or bond indices (e.g., Bloomberg Global Benchmark Bond Indices). An investment with a beta of 1 will increase and decrease in market price at the exact same rates as the average of the entire market. An investment with a beta greater than 1 will increase and decrease in returns much more severely—it will be very volatile—making it appear very risky according to CAPM, even if it consistently over-performs compared to the market. An investment with a beta of less than 1 will be very stable and will not change its rate of return very much, making it appear safe according to CAPM, even if that rate of return is consistently lower than the market average. Beta just doesn't function as a measurement of risk—its only purpose is to measure volatility compared to the market average—but it is commonly used incorrectly, so it's worth knowing how to interpret the information being used.

Instead of using beta, measurements of risk are now mostly based in another model known as 'arbitrage pricing theory' (APT). The core APT model doesn't really tell you anything about risk at all; it's just a framework that people use to develop and customize their own calculations of risk, which include any of a number of variables that the individual investor has determined contribute to risk.

While APT models of risk analysis can be extremely useful, they also tend to require a high degree of expertise. Models of risk that are more common, due to their relative simplicity, are value at risk (VaR) and expected shortfall (ES). These are statistical methods which refer to the likelihood of losses to determine the maximum amount of likely losses. Say, for example, you want to be 99 per cent certain of the potential losses of a given risky event, then by estimating your probability of loss (generally using historical information), you can determine the maximum amount of losses you can expect with 99 per cent certainty (this is your VaR). There are multiple implications of this. First, once you know the maximum amount of losses you can sustain and still have an overall gain, you can estimate the maximum amount of risk you can incur. Second, it allows you to manage the amount of total risk incurred between multiple investments or clients in a portfolio, so that the total risk does not exceed a given value, or so that any single item does not exceed a given risk value.

KEY TERMS

Value at risk (VaR): An estimation of the maximum amount of financial losses likely to be experienced.

Expected shortfall (ES): An estimation of the maximum amount of financial losses that could potentially be experienced, though unlikely.

VaR, in its original format, has some limitations which critics say lead people to incur greater risk than necessary, which is why many people prefer expected shortfall (ES), which estimates how bad things can get in the worst-case scenario. In other words, it calculates the expected losses within the 1 per cent range. This accounts for one of the shortcomings of VaR; for example, a portfolio in which 99 per cent of items have a very low probability of loss could still have 1 per cent of items that are likely to have dramatic losses. Expected shortfall seeks to manage the amount of maximum risk incurred.

Even more popular than VaR and ES, again due to the fact that they are even simpler to use, are the ratings given to investments by underwriting agencies (see p. 70). They will rate each risk on a custom scale, such as AAA, AA+, AA, etc. Though commonly used, these rating systems have fallen into question after the 2008 financial collapse, since many of the investments now considered 'toxic' (a high credit risk) were given higher ratings than they deserved, with speculation of collaboration between agencies and major banks.

RISK MANAGEMENT

There are a number of ways to limit the amount of risk to which your finances are exposed, each with their own strengths and weaknesses, and the trick to successful risk management is knowing when it is appropriate to use each.

Diversification

One of the most commonly cited methods for managing financial risk is through diversification, the goal of which is to make sure that any losses you experience are offset by gains. If you put all your money in a single investment, and that investment loses value, then you could lose everything, but if you put your money in two investments known for moving in opposite directions (historically, as one loses value, the other tends to increase in value), then your total wealth will improve in stability. Diversifying your money among several investments can limit the impact of specific risks on your investments, but not the impact of market risk. To diversify away market risk, it's necessary to buy investments in a variety of different countries; as shown in the post-2008 era wherein many Western countries struggled economically, but investments in many Asian countries continued to show stable growth. This is not only true with investments, but with income as well—if you are self-employed or entrepreneurial and accept many different clients, then if you need to end your relationship with one of those clients, you can still rely on the others while you seek additional work. By contrast, while working for one employer, if things go wrong, then you will find yourself in a very desperate situation; even if you don't lose your job, your negotiating power in the labour markets is diminished, as you have less leverage during negotiations than your employer. As the old saying goes, 'don't put all your eggs in one basket'.

THINK ABOUT IT

The world's two most famous investors, Warren Buffett and Charlie Munger, say that diversification is for people who don't know what they are doing. The logic goes like this: you are always going to pick the best investment first, and diversification requires you to choose a variety of different investments, so that you become invested not just in your top choice, but in your second choice, third choice and possibly others which aren't as good as your top choice. It's the opinion of Warren and Charlie that a person should simply allocate all their funds to their best choice of investment and earn the highest return possible. It's prudent to note, however, that Berkshire Hathaway (the outlet through which Warren and Charlie make their investments) is invested in well over 100 different companies, which is far above even highly diversified portfolios.

Derivatives

The derivatives market actually began as a way to help stabilize finances and production for farmers, ranchers and others who work in agriculture. The supply of these seasonal goods plummets during off-season, causing prices to soar until harvest season, at which point there's a surplus of these goods that can be difficult to sell at all, much less receive a reasonable price for, since everyone is fighting over buyers. The result used to be that all these farmers would come to market with their goods, sell what they could for a pittance, and then before going back home they would dump the surplus into the street. This was common practice until derivatives were invented, specifically, futures contracts into which two parties entered as an obligation to exchange a specific volume of a specific product for a specific price. This alone helped to stabilize the agricultural markets, but once people realized they could start buying and selling the contracts themselves, as one would equities, the commodities exchange markets were born. The popularity of these markets attracted people from other industries such as stocks to incorporate these derivatives contracts in non-commodity sectors, and now they can literally be used for just about any type of exchange you can imagine. They have three basic purposes:

1. Economic stabilization: As discussed, the use of derivatives reduces price and production volatility.
2. Risk management: With guarantees in the volume and price of assets being purchased, the risk of losses is largely mitigated.
3. Speculation: A lot of people use derivatives to generate revenue by speculating on future movements of market price (buying or selling derivatives with the expectation that the market will move against the other person, or buying then reselling them), which has raised concerns regarding the potential to manipulate markets using derivatives, or illegally hide losses.

INSURANCE

Besides simply limiting the amount of risk to which you are exposed, there's also a way to share that risk with others who are in a similar situation: insurance.

The idea behind buying insurance is that you could experience a large financial loss, so you pay the insurance company periodic payments called 'premiums', and the insurance company is obligated to pay for your losses if they occur. The insurance company knows the exact probability that you will incur those losses, and it knows how much it must charge each person to continue to make a profit. Basically, lots of people buy insurance, and only a few of them will experience losses, so the money that everyone else pays in premiums covers the cost of those losses, plus the amount of the company's profits and operating costs. Statistically, this means that everyone is overpaying for the cost of this risk, on the grounds that if they do experience losses, they will not be completely devastated. Many countries realize that the insurance industry represents a major price distortion and provide nationalized services, such as health care, that would otherwise require insurance. Even among other types of insurance, being insured is not a guarantee against financial devastation, as people still statistically benefit more from paying out-of-pocket for these expenses than buying insurance.

So why do people buy insurance at all? As with all financial decisions, whether or not to buy insurance is not one that can be made for you, because each person's circumstances are different, and for those who do experience a devastating loss, insurance can mean the difference between financial stability and collapse. The question becomes a personal one—how risk-averse you are, your own perceived likelihood of loss and what you are willing to pay in order to avoid loss.

DUE DILIGENCE

In the end, the best tool you have available to you in limiting the costs associated with risk is simple due diligence. Do your research, make decisions which make sense to you, and keep watching so you know when that decision doesn't make sense anymore. If someone's credibility is in question, risk mitigation can come in forms as simple as asking for a nonrefundable down-payment, just as banks will sometimes ask for collateral before issuing loans. Preparing for losses can be as simple as keeping enough funds available in a liquid form so you can pay your bills until you regain your losses. The duration of your exposure to losses can be shortened by ensuring you always have an exit strategy—before you commit to a decision, develop a way to undo it in a worst-case scenario. Like most things, you get out of risk management what you put into it, and as the amount of potential risk increases, so should your intolerance for sloppy risk management.

– 8 –

INCOME

Many people use the words 'wages' and 'income' interchangeably, but your wages—the money you earn from being employed—are only a single source of income. People forget that there are a variety of sources of income and become entirely dependent on just their wages, putting them in a risky financial position and a disadvantageous position when negotiating their wages. In this chapter we will explore a variety of common sources of income and how they can be managed to your benefit.

INCOME DIVERSIFICATION

The very wealthy make only about 30–40 per cent of their total income from their wages. The remainder of their income comes from other sources. Most others depend on their wages as their sole source of income. When this is the case, the idea of losing that income is unbearable, and if you do, you become desperate to replace it with anything you can find. This puts you in a weak position to negotiate wages, since you are incapable or unwilling to demand more, and unable to dedicate the time to finding better work. You end up spending the majority of your earnings on subsistence goods and the repayment of debts, while your financial fate is entirely in the hands of an employer who has little or no obligation to retain you. Little or nothing is passed on to your children, and since you have no practice with investing or financial management, the decisions you make will likely be less than optimal, and your kids will have difficulty learning these skills, making many of the same mistakes.

So, how do you avoid falling into this trap? This is all connected to differences in marginal propensity to consume (MPC) and marginal propensity to save (MPS). MPC is the proportion of your total income that you spend, while MPS is the proportion of your total income that you save. If you maintain a single income stream (and a weak negotiating position in the labour markets), you will have difficulty decreasing your MPC, so will end up spending a large percentage of your income on survival goods. Diversify your income by pursuing several different sources and you will be in a stronger financial position should any of those sources of income fail. You will be able to dedicate the time to replacing it, you won't have as much pressure to accept whatever wage is being offered, and you may even have an opportunity to test new sources of income, such as going self-employed.

KEY TERMS

Marginal propensity to consume: The proportion of total income that is spent.

Marginal propensity to save: The proportion of total income that is saved.

Common sources of income

Income comes from a large variety of sources; some of the more common sources that you might use to diversify your income include:

- Wages—This is the money you earn from being employed. Wages accumulate at regular intervals, generally either hourly, monthly or annually, and are typically paid weekly, biweekly or monthly. The rate at which you are paid is negotiated between you and your employer, although many countries have laws in place guaranteeing a minimum wage that is regularly adjusted with the cost of living.

- Royalties—If you have ever created something that is copied for mass production and sold, you will likely earn royalties. This is the money you earn when you write a book, record music, make a movie and so forth. For example, if you are reading this book, then I have earned a percentage of the price you paid for it. (Thank you!) The amount of royalties you receive are negotiated in advance and are included in a contract, and you will continue to earn them indefinitely, so long as the thing you made keeps selling. It is also common to receive an advance against royalties, which means that you are given money in advance, and you won't receive any more until the total royalties you have earned exceeds the amount of your advance.

- Investment/Banking income—Many types of investments yield income. Bank accounts frequently offer interest, as do bonds; annuities and preferred stock both offer guaranteed regular income; common stock sometimes offers dividend income as well. Simply by investing in these things, the money you save will not just increase in value, but will actually become an additional source of income.

- Business income—If you own a business, are self-employed or own farmland, this will be a source of income for you. It is the goal of entrepreneurs to own several businesses and hire effective managers so that they can retire and simply collect the income from the success of these businesses. If you own operations such as this, you are entitled to the profits that compose your income.

- Government benefits income—There is often a stigma attached to receiving government benefits, as people worry about fraud or the shirking of active employment necessary to sustain yourself financially. The reality, though, as shown time and again in a variety of studies, is that these cases are a very small minority of total benefits recipients. These programmes were put into place for a reason—during the Great Depression of the 1930s, economists proved that programmes like these were required to support the consumer base that drives national production and employment. So, if you legitimately meet the criteria to receive benefits under one of these programmes, the nation's overall economic health depends on your taking advantage of it.

- Alimony/Child support—If you have been married and have separated and your partner was the wage-earner upon whom you were dependent for your finances, or you had become accustomed to a certain lifestyle that you cannot accomplish on your own, you may be legally entitled to alimony—money that the other person is legally obligated to give you in order to continue supporting your finances. Child support works in a similar fashion. If the other parent of your child refuses to assist financially with raising the child, the courts may require them to give you money.

- Jury duty pay—If you are called to be on the jury of a trial, many countries will compensate you for any days of work you have lost.

- Winnings—If you win money for any reason, this also contributes to your income. For the majority of people, winnings constitute a one-time event which will only impact their income in that year, and not significantly. Some people win a large enough amount that they will receive payments for an extended period of time, and others make a successful career gambling.

- Legal damages—If you have been wronged, purposefully or accidentally, you may be legally entitled to receive regular payments from the person who wronged you in order to assist you with the costs and hardships that have resulted.
- Gifts/Inheritances—If someone gives you money and they are still alive, it's considered a gift; if they give you money as a part of their will, it's an inheritance.
- Grants/Scholarships—When a person or organization gives you money to achieve a specific goal, such as attending university, this contributes to your income. Typically, the money from grants and scholarships must be used in specific ways; scholarships are often given directly to the university; research grants generally require you to detail your use of funds in the application. Still, these help to fund your expenses.
- Retirement income—See chapter 9.
- Profits from the sale of assets—If you have bought something and were fortunate enough to sell it for a higher price than you paid, the difference is considered a profit that contributes to your income. This may mean a one-time sale of some high-value asset, or it may mean that you do a lot of antiquing, reselling eBay auction items or some other activity that allows you to generate small but regular profits.

NOMINAL VS. REAL INCOME

We measure the value of the goods we buy in terms of the *volume* of money we must give in exchange for them, but at the same time we measure the *value* of money in terms of what we are able to acquire in exchange for it. Money has no intrinsic value—it is a measure of debt value which facilitates bartered exchanges. When you go to work and earn wages, it is likely that you don't want what your employer offers, so instead your employer gives you a kind of IOU, allowing you to acquire goods from others in exchange for the IOU. As more people honour the same type of IOU, it becomes more valuable and more stable. Currencies, gold, cigarettes in prison and cryptocurrencies like Bitcoin are all virtually useless except as a measurement of the value of the exchanges for which they are being used. So, every time you make a purchase, you are indirectly assessing what your purchase is worth in terms of the amount of work you would have to give your employer. The total value of production underlying the volume of a given currency will largely define the value of each unit of that currency. For a number of reasons, the volume of currency we must pay to acquire goods slowly increases over time, or the amount of stuff a single unit of currency can buy—its purchasing power—decreases. This is known as inflation. At the same time that people are paying more to purchase things, they are also (usually) earning more for the work they do, which means that everyone is paying more money in terms of volume, but the same in terms of percentage of the money they make at work.

KEY TERMS

Purchasing power: The ability of a fiat currency to be exchanged for goods and services.

Inflation: A reduction in the purchasing power of a currency.

This is the difference between nominal and real income. Nominal income is the volume of money you receive. Whatever your income was for the year, that's your nominal income. Real income, by contrast, is the amount of purchasing power you earn—it's the amount of stuff you can buy. Clearly this isn't very useful in financial planning, so rather than attempting to list all the stuff you can buy, we use your nominal income adjusted for inflation. For example, take whatever your income is this year and then decrease that amount by 2 per cent each year into the future, because in our example your income will lose 2 per cent of its purchasing power each year to inflation. That is, of course, assuming your income doesn't increase during that time period. In a more realistic scenario, you would decrease the value of your income by whatever the inflation rate was during the past year, which is easy to find by searching online sources such as the World Bank website, which publicly publishes such data. You can't guarantee with 100 per cent certainty that your employer will increase your wages with the cost of living, so in order to guarantee the value of your wealth and your income, you need to respond to the forces of inflation.

Since inflation causes the value of your bank account to decrease over time in terms of the amount of stuff you will be able to buy, you need to make sure that the money you have is earning interest rates at least as high as the inflation rate. If your wages don't increase at least with the cost of living, continue to pursue other sources of income or switch companies to one that offers higher wages. Continue to track inflation as well as the rates of return and increased value of your various sources of income to make sure that your wealth and income both remain intact.

PERSONAL STATEMENT OF CASH FLOWS

'Cash flow' refers to any movement of money, whether you are earning it or spending it. Any time the amount of money that you have changes for any reason, it's a cash flow; when you earn it, that's a positive cash flow, and when you lose it, that's a negative cash flow. Your personal income statement (discussed in chapter 2) describes your overall revenues and costs so you can determine how much money you are making, and your personal balance sheet (discussed in chapter 6) describes the value of your assets and debt. Neither of these helps you to identify the activities in which you participate that create cash flows, or what you can do to improve them. For that, we refer to the personal statement of cash flows, which fills the remaining gaps in your financial records to show where the positive and negative changes to your cash are occurring.

TRY IT NOW! The statement of cash flows is easier to understand once you put one together, so let's do one now.

Operating activities

Cash inflows

Item 1 $XX.xx

Item 2 $XX.xx

Cash outflows

Item 1 $XX.xx

Item 2 $XX.xx

Investing activities

Cash inflows

Item 1 $XX.xx

Item 2 $XX.xx

Cash outflows

Item 1 $XX.xx

Item 2 $XX.xx

Financing activities

Cash inflows

Item 1 $XX.xx

Item 2 $XX.xx

Cash outflows

Item 1 $XX.xx

Item 2 $XX.xx

Each of the three categories (operating, investing, and financing) refers to a different type of cash flow activity. Operating activities are those associated with your primary employment—the things you do to earn money, and the money you spend on subsistence and consumption, including morale expenditures like entertainment. Operating inflows include any sources of money you earn and should each be listed individually, including the amount earned from each source for the period. Operating outflows include anything on which you spend money. Investing activities refers to anything you do associated with investing; inflows are the money you earn through investing income or the sale of investments, and outflows include any money you spend to purchase investments or that you lose to poor investments. As with operating activities, list each source of both inflows and outflows, and their value for the period. Finally, financing activities refers to any activities associated with debt used to finance operations or investments. Financing inflows include any money borrowed, and outflows include interest and principal payments.

The statement of cash flows is not only an important tool in managing your sources of income and managing your income diversification, but also provides critical information which elaborates on the other financial statements discussed in this book.

– 9 –

RETIREMENT PLANNING

There comes a time in every person's life that they want to, should or must focus on enriching their lives rather than their finances or career. One of the biggest challenges to achieving this is financial—developing a plan that will financially prepare you to eliminate dependency on your employer. As discussed in chapter 8, for most people, the primary source of their income is their career, which means that they must develop a plan to survive and thrive as they pursue self-actualization rather than income. For these individuals, the costs of living and the pursuit of enriching activities are funded not with wages generated through labour, but with the wealth they have accumulated over a lifetime of said labour. Wealth is the difference between how much you make and how much you spend: in other words, all the money and assets you accumulate over the course of your lifetime, whether it's cash in the bank, property or business ownership, or physical possessions. Over the course of this chapter, we explore different strategies for accumulating wealth for retirement, how to maximize your quality of life during retirement, and how to make plans to pass the torch to the next generation.

RETIREMENT ACCOUNTS

Many countries have laws regarding accounts intended for people to save for retirement. Although savings accounts intended for this purpose do exist, more often than not these are brokerage accounts (both discussed on p. 36), since people saving for retirement benefit more from investing their funds and allowing them to increase in value, rather than letting them sit in a bank account earning tiny amounts of interest. Retirement accounts are given preferential tax status: either contributions to the account are exempt from income tax but added value earned by investing the money is taxed when it is withdrawn, or the income itself is taxed before being put into the account but the value it earns through investing is tax free upon withdrawal, or both. Some retirement accounts are available only to people in specific careers or sectors, or to the self-employed, and each type will have its own unique name and legal regulations. If you plan on opening a retirement account, check with your bank to see what options they have available for you.

Retirement accounts: Accounts that are given preferential tax status when specific criteria towards retirement are met.

If you use the money in the account before the specified retirement age, those funds will generally lose their tax status and you will have to pay a tax penalty on them, although sometimes there are exemptions if they are used for qualifying reasons such as emergency expenses. It's also frequently possible to borrow against your retirement account, so that you can have access to the funds without the tax penalties, but you are required to pay it back within a specified period of time. If you absolutely must access these funds early, ensure that you carefully consider the costs associated with doing so, and the impact that it will have on your future retirement plans. There are scarce few opportunities for which it will be worth the cost.

HOW MUCH SHOULD YOU SAVE?

Before you can decide the best method of saving for retirement, you need to figure out exactly how much you will need. This is a question that seems simple on the surface but quickly becomes difficult to answer, because there are a lot of unknowns to consider. It's not enough to multiply the amount you spend every year by the number of years you plan to live, because your bills will change over that period, the length of your life is uncertain, the investments you make will change their value, you will alter the types of investments you hold, and even the value of the money itself will change. If you are feeling a little overwhelmed already, you are not alone—many people aren't certain how to answer this question, much less determine how they will achieve savings goals based on it. The good news is that although there are many things to consider, no individual item is at all difficult; so if we go step-by-step, you should have absolutely no problem.

Step one: The first thing to ask yourself is how much money you will need to pay off your major debts—mortgage, car loans, medical or student bills, etc. If your current situation is not the one you intend to keep, then determine how much you are going to need to cover your expenses prior to, during and after the transition. The goal of this step is to create an estimate of how much you will need to spend in order to get to retirement.

Step two: Try to determine how long you can expect to live. There's no denying this is a morbid subject that makes many people uncomfortable, but without some estimate of the length of your life, it's impossible to makes plans for that life. There are a variety of factors to consider when estimating your age expectations, such as the average lifespan of people in your family, the average life expectancy of people in your country and any health variables that are likely to lengthen or shorten your life expectancy compared to the people around you. Any estimate is, of course, not guaranteed, so it's best to be liberal—whatever your best estimate is, add 10–15 years, just to be on the safe side. Another method is to simply plan to reach age 100—it's a nice, round number that's easy to use when doing calculations, and the probability of exceeding age 100 is very low, so it's also a safe estimate.

Step three: Consider what your cost of living will be after you retire. Exactly what is it you plan to do after retirement, and what will it cost to sustain that lifestyle? A common reference point to use in determining this is to estimate what it will cost to sustain your current lifestyle, not including any expenses that will be paid off by that point, and then include the costs of the ventures you intend to pursue. This will be your 'ideal retirement scenario', which will set an upper limit on the amount you will need for retirement. Another common reference point is the estimate of what it would cost to live minimally—the total annual expenses you will incur just to meet your most basic survival requirements. While this should not be your goal (for reasons discussed later in this chapter), it does give you the lower limit on the amount you will need. Then, within the upper and lower limits, you can see how many years it would take to save enough money using your current income, or how much money you would have to make in order to retire at a given age. This will help to shape your goals for age and style of retirement, as well as for your income, expenses and savings.

THINK ABOUT IT

Don't simply plan for a sedentary retirement that only allows you to meet your basic survival needs. Retirement presents the opportunity to pursue personal goals, so ask yourself what it means to *live*, instead of just *existing*. Many people work their whole life in order to support a spouse and children, and retirement presents an opportunity to plan family activities and spend time with grandchildren. Other people take the opportunity to travel and learn more about the world, exposing themselves to new philosophies and cultures. Some people write about their experiences, teach at local universities or guide others pursuing similar paths as a consultant, finding happiness in helping others to learn from what they have accomplished. Others learn new skills which provide a creative outlet. Whatever it is that motivates you to succeed—include it in your retirement plan. Estimate the costs associated with it and include them in your financial goals. Your plans for retirement may change, but saving for one plan will put you on the correct path for any plan, though perhaps not as precisely as originally intended.

Step four: A reality of our increasing life expectancies is that many people require more assistance in their old age. That may mean medical treatments or equipment to improve the quality of your life, or the cost of living in sheltered accommodation or a nursing home. Sometimes people expect that their families will take care of them, but often this is undesirable or otherwise not possible, and there are some complex illnesses, such as dementia, for which your average family just isn't prepared (unless you have a lot of doctors or nurses in the family, in which case it may be an option, but is something you should talk to them about ahead of time). Choose the style and quality of care you would want, determine the expenses associated with it, and consider if switching to your back-up plans will eliminate any expenses associated with your primary plans. Set your financial goals to meet whichever plan is most expensive.

Finally, there's the issue of inflation. Things cost more than they used to, but people also make more than they used to, so in the end it all tends to even out, on average (discussed more on pp. 115–17). The problem is that once you retire, your income has a tendency to stop adjusting for inflation, so you can't use the costs you have today as a fair estimate of the costs you will have over the duration of your retirement. Inflation growth rates, over the long term, tend to grow at a relatively stable pace, following certain economic cycles (which will be discussed later in this chapter). So, whatever the average inflation rate is in the area you plan to retire, expect that it will continue indefinitely and that the prices of everything associated with your retirement will increase at that rate each year.

REMEMBER THIS!!! It's better to have a plan and not need it, than to need a plan and not have it. Whatever your ideal arrangements for retirement, make sure you have a back-up plan.

SOURCES OF RETIREMENT INCOME

Many countries have governmental financial assistance programmes for retired people. Although it makes complete sense, from a strictly financial perspective, to take advantage of these programmes, not all countries have them, and it's not always prudent to assume that such programmes will continue to be available when you are ready to retire. (That depends on the political climate over the years, and politics tends to be . . . well, *inconsistent* is the nice word for it.) As the goal of retirement is to become truly financially independent, let's focus on ways to fund your retirement that you can actively pursue.

The first, and most common, source of retirement income is the money people save over the course of their employment. Recall from chapter 6 that your assets don't necessarily just increase their value, to be sold at a later date, but they can also generate income. If you own one or more businesses, managed by people you trust, you can continue to collect income from their profits indefinitely without requiring you to do any work. If you own farmland, then as long as it is productive, it's possible to hire people to manage it and to collect income from its produce. The same is true of real estate—you can lease buildings or commercially viable land and hire someone to manage it, generating income for you. If you have ever written a book, been in a movie or recorded music, it's likely you will receive royalty income twice a year for an extended period of time, gradually diminishing as sales slow. These all tend to be career-oriented sources of income, though, rather than broadly available investments.

There are also a few different types of investments that generate income without requiring their sale. These investments are available to anyone, and are divided into two broad categories: fixed-income and variable-income investments.

Fixed-income investments

These investments are contractually obligated to pay you a guaranteed amount of income at predetermined intervals over the life of the investment. Annuities, for example, are specifically designed for that purpose—you pay regular premiums, as you would with an insurance policy, but for a given period of time, and once the annuity matures, you will stop making payments and will begin to receive payments. There is an immense variety of annuities available, which range in the amount of income they pay, their price, their duration, and so forth. You can even purchase additional features, called 'riders', which can offer a lump-sum payment or continue payments to a surviving beneficiary after your death. It is in the nature of annuities that the more you pay and the longer you pay it, the more you will receive in return.

Bonds are another form of fixed-income investment which either pay in a lump sum or in increments called 'coupons' (see chapter 6 for discussion of coupons, preferred stock and asset-backed securities). Preferred equities are just like common stocks, except equity holders don't get voting rights; they do get preferential status if the company goes out of business and liquidates everything, and, more importantly, they pay a guaranteed dividend. Asset-backed securities also pay a guaranteed income, as the underlying asset earns revenues, such as mortgage repayments—the revenues from which are distributed to the owners of the securities that funded the mortgage in the first place.

These investments all offer a guaranteed value and income at fixed intervals and provide certainty and a degree of safety when planning for retirement that can't be replicated with variable-income investments. However, they also offer less opportunity for those who are less risk-averse.

KEY TERMS

Annuity: A financial product similar to insurance, but which functions as an income-generating investment rather than a risk management tool.

Riders: Contractual additions to an annuity that can be purchased for an additional fee.

Variable-income investments

The income generated from variable-income investments may or may not be guaranteed, depending on the type of investment, but the value of that income will fluctuate. For example, variable annuities work just like other annuities, but the amount of money you receive on each payment will depend on how effectively the money has been invested by the insurance company from which you bought the annuity. In other words, any time you make premium payments to the insurance company for an annuity, they invest that money and—with variable annuities—the performance of those investments will determine how much money you make. Hybrid-income

investments combine elements of both fixed-income and variable-income investments, generally exclusive to annuities. These allow the investor to pick what percentage of their annuity should be fixed and what percentage should be variable, ensuring that they receive a guaranteed minimum income, with the potential to earn more.

Unlike preferred equities, common equities are not obligated to pay a dividend. Companies that do pay a dividend will tend to do so consistently, but the amount paid will depend on the company's profits. Since shareholders are the owners of the company, the profits technically belong to them, but whether or not you earn dividends depends entirely on company performance and intentions for growth.

Another source of income commonly used to fund retirement is the reverse mortgage. If you own your home and have fully repaid your original mortgage, then you can get a reverse mortgage. The reverse mortgage means that the bank will buy your house from you, but allow you to continue living there for the remainder of your life. The bank puts a lien on the property as collateral, with the expectation that you will not repay the money but, rather, let them take the property when you are finished with it. What you do with the money from your reverse mortgage is completely up to you, but it's prudent to note that your surviving beneficiaries will *not* receive the property—if you have any money remaining, they will receive that, but not the property.

KEY TERM **Reverse mortgage**: A type of home equity loan in which the lender takes the house after the borrower dies in lieu of loan repayment.

One type of retirement income, a bit different from the others, is long-term care insurance. This is different because it is technically insurance, rather than true income, which means that you will receive funding assistance for specific types of care you might receive, rather

than receiving income based on the value of an asset. As with any other type of insurance, you pay a regular premium for long-term care insurance and then any qualifying costs you incur for long-term care will be paid for by the insurance company. Generally this means care costs which surpass the duration, price or type covered by normal health insurance, and only those associated with caring for people during their retirement. While this does provide a method of funding retirement expenses, remember that this income is only guaranteed if certain criteria are met.

Diversification of income during retirement can be critical to the stability of that income. No different than with investments (discussed in chapter 6) or income (discussed in chapter 8), diversification of your retirement income reduces the amount of risk you will experience during a time of life when appetite for risk should be at its lowest point.

ECONOMIC CYCLES

The value of assets such as stocks and real estate increases on average over the long run, but it also tends to fluctuate in waves—it will go up for a while, then down a little, then up some more and down again. If you are not careful these waves can make you seasick, metaphorically speaking, of course. If you watch these cycles happen but aren't aware of how to manage your response, you could find yourself making poor financial decisions as a result, or even attempting to retire shortly after a devastating economic collapse, as happened to many people after the 2008 financial collapse. There are ways to prevent this from happening.

The main thing to consider is your 'time horizon'—the number of years you have remaining before your planned retirement date.

When you are young and first begin saving for retirement, it's easy to take a lot of risk without worrying about cyclical losses, because you think you will have more than enough time to regain that value. This is a mistake a lot of people make, as they sell all their investments when the economy crashes, forgetting that economies eventually recover. A recession is the worst time to sell your investments because you will get the worst possible price for them, for the reason of a national economic cycle rather than anything inherent to the investments themselves. It is important, however, that you don't confuse economic cycles with troubled investments; if your investments are doing poorly in a strong economy, consistently underperform or otherwise give you reason to believe that the price won't recover, then don't stay on a sinking ship—sell those investments and buy something better. Losses resulting from economic cycles, such as recessions, will recover; so remain persistent. After you get some practice and become familiar with these cycles, you can even sell your investments just as they begin and then rebuy them when they lose a lot of their value, maximizing your wealth. Another approach is to buy more investments slowly as their price drops, and then to sell them again slowly as their price recovers. This reduces some of the risk associated with the economy's uncertain movements—something which so many people struggle to predict, even experts.

If you know how to ride these cyclical waves in the economy, you can actually use them to your advantage, but even if you just hold onto your investments and wait out the recession, you will regain the value eventually. These cycles only really pose a risk to people who are getting ready to retire in the middle of one. This is why you should absolutely manage a shift in the types of investments you hold as you get closer to your retirement. When you are young, more volatile investments like equity index funds will give you the highest growth rates, even though the price roller coaster may make you dizzy. As you get closer to your retirement date, the timing of these cycles can be very unfortunate, leaving you with little money to fund your retirement; so over the years you should gradually switch from high-risk to low-risk investments. This means that you should regularly increase the percentage of your total investments that are allocated to things like low-risk bonds, fixed-rate annuities or even high-yield bank accounts. That way, by the time you are ready to retire, the fluctuations in the economy will have little influence on the value of your investments. This process of gradual risk reduction will help to give you the highest returns on your investments, while carefully managing the amount of risk to which you are exposed.

PASSING THE TORCH

You are going to have to figure out what will happen to your finances when they are no longer of use to you. Nothing is forcing you to make that decision, but if you don't, it will be made for you in accordance with the laws in your country, and that may result in actions contrary to what you would prefer. So, it's best to make your wishes known through a will.

Everything that you leave behind, whether wealth or debt, is considered your 'estate'. Making preparations for what will happen to your estate when you die can be a very complicated process, so I strongly recommend using the services of a professional who specializes in estate planning (typically a legal or financial professional dedicated specifically to estate services). They will guide you through the laws in your country that concern the wording of your will, the rights of those who inherit your wealth or debt, and how to minimize the tax impact on your beneficiaries. Besides the distribution of your assets, three financial products are available to ensure that your surviving family continues to receive income support: annuities with survivorship riders (discussed earlier in this chapter), life insurance policies and trusts.

There are two broad types of life insurance: term and whole. Term life insurance is simple—you are thoroughly evaluated in order to determine the price of your premiums, and, so long as you consistently pay those premiums without letting your policy lapse, the policy will remain the same indefinitely, until your survivors file a claim and receive the insurance benefits. Whole life is a little different; you still pay premiums, and your survivors still get insurance benefits once they file the claim, but whole life actually accumulates in value over time. As you pay your premiums, they contribute to the current cash value of the policy and continue to do so until that value reaches the value of the claim benefits, at which point, even if you are still alive, you receive the money, because any additional payments would actually be more than what anyone would receive. Since there is a cash value to these policies, you can borrow against them or even sell the policy back to the insurance company for its cash value, minus a substantial penalty. Regardless of the type of life insurance you choose, your beneficiaries can choose payments over time or a lump sum, and you generally also have the option to reinvest the money into an annuity and receive annuity income instead.

Trusts are a little different from annuities or insurance. Trusts are a special type of brokerage account into which funds are deposited and invested, and a third party manages the account while your beneficiaries receive benefits from it—either receiving the total value of the trust when specific requirements which you set are met, or continuously receiving the investment income from that account.

Something to consider when planning to pass on your estate is the costs your beneficiaries will incur in managing your remains. Burial or cremation must be purchased and can be extremely expensive, depending on the options chosen. Make sure to take into consideration the regulations of your country before settling on an option. One option that is much cheaper, and which can save the lives of others, is to donate your body. Often there are transplant patients who desperately need a new heart, liver or kidney, but cannot find a donor. Other times donated bodies are used in medical research to find cures or discover new techniques that will save the lives of people in the future. This decision is, of course, a very personal one, but from a purely financial perspective, donation is the cheapest option. Around the world, survivors generally also have a funeral ceremony, gathering together to celebrate your memory and provide closure—the cost of which can vary greatly, depending on the location, decorations, catering, music, etc.

– 10 –

BEHAVIOURAL FINANCE

People have a tendency to believe that their financial decisions are rational, based on empirical evidence of calculated analysis, and, since finance is a highly quantitative field, it is reasonable to think that this is true. However, more often than not, actual decisions—made even by experienced experts—are determined by psychology rather than finances. These psychological traits are the result of millennia of physiological and behavioural evolution, but only since the 1970s have we been aware of the way in which they cause our financial actions to deviate so greatly from what is considered 'rational'. That's not to say the irrational paradigm of finance is illogical, since these behaviours are quite beneficial within the contexts in which they evolved, but as they were never intended to allow us to improve our financial decisions, it becomes vital to understand how our minds tend to hijack our money management.

HERD BEHAVIOUR

One of the most well-known psychological anomalies of finance is known as 'herd behaviour' and is generally illustrated as a cliché about a securities trader loudly placing an order, followed by a chorus of others placing similar orders. There's a lot of truth in this example; quite frequently investors will place orders simply because they believe everyone else is doing the same thing. This may sound absurd, but imagine for a moment that you are on a busy street minding your own business when, suddenly, everyone around you starts running, panicked, in one direction. Odds are that you will feel compelled to run with them, since waiting around to see what you are running from may come with a considerable degree of risk. Within this context, it's easy to see how herd behaviour evolved as a survival instinct. In finance, particularly when managing investments that have a high degree of risk (such as equities), it's common for people to see others taking a particular action and to wonder whether those people know something not immediately evident. Some high-profile investors will actually charge a subscription fee for the privilege of being notified of purchases or sales in their portfolios so that the subscribers can do the same. Investment bubbles are most commonly caused by herd behaviour, as the market price of a particular class of assets (e.g., internet stocks during the 'dot com bubble', real estate during the 2008 financial collapse) rapidly increases as major investment funds make purchases, causing a chain reaction of people investing in the same investments simply because it is trendy, rather than because of anything to do with the value of the assets themselves. Even in consumer purchases, sometimes people feel obligated to socially compete with the clothes they wear or the car they drive, or to make home improvements so as not to appear inferior to neighbours (colloquially known as 'keeping up with the Joneses'). This type of stampede isn't caused by the threat of financial loss but, rather, loss of esteem.

Although all people will experience herd behaviour at some point in their lives, it's important not to let it influence your financial decisions. Each person's finances are unique, so a decision that is right for one person will not be right for every person, and there is always the distinct possibility that the people around you don't know what they are doing. As we live in a dynamic, ever-changing world, even the circumstances in which a given decision was made will not be exactly the same by the time you have an opportunity to mimic it. By the time you notice that it's popular to invest in a particular industry, the market price of those investments may have already surpassed their value, or those investments may be more speculative than is appropriate for your time horizon. There is no reason to buy a Maserati just because your colleague has one, and the possibility exists that your colleague is drowning in debt after buying it or lives in a smaller home so that they can afford it. The actions of others can be a great place to begin looking for leads on what to do with your money, but can only give you enough information to research options, not make decisions.

REMEMBER THIS!!! The rule of thumb in managing herd behaviour is this: seek what is rational, not a rationalization.

SATISFICING

Behavioural models of finance are expressed in terms of deviations from rationality, wherein each financial challenge you face has an optimal response which can be calculated, with psychological phenomena causing a measurable deviation from that optimal response. This has some interesting implications when looking at a psychological behaviour known as 'satisficing'. Until recently, all financial, consumer and other economic models were based on the assumption that all people sought to optimize their asset utilization, but these failed to take into account the value that people place on their time and effort. Rather than fully satisfying one's needs for any particular financial activity, people 'satisfice'.

Satisficing refers to a person's propensity to accept what is sufficient, or 'good enough'. To some, this may sound like negligence, but in most situations there is a point wherein the benefits of allocating additional time or resources become too small for justification. For example, having perfect information means being paralyzed with indecision, and people function in their daily lives by learning to identify and evaluate the most important information, and leaving the rest to judgement and assumptions. When shopping for groceries, people tend to choose a favourite store that most consistently meets their needs, at which point they no longer research the prices of every store for every item they purchase, because the minuscule amount of money they could potentially save is depleted on transportation and time which could be better used. Every decision we make is weighted not only against the alternative options, but also against inaction, as we ask ourselves: 'Is it worth it?'

As with all financial behaviours, it is possible to measure the value of satisficing by comparing the value of the decision made against the value of the optimum decision. For example, if you were to purchase tea at the nearest store for its convenience, then determine that the next nearest store sells the same tea for 1 per cent less, then the cost of satisficing is 1 percent of the price of tea. That's because the decision which optimizes the value of your tea is to go to the farther store, since paying less money for equal benefit yields greater value for the money spent. This allows for a rough estimate of the value people put on their own time and effort; when buying a car, people do a lot more research to find the best value than they do with something cheap like tea, since the amount of money which could potentially be saved is much greater when buying big-ticket items. At any given time, you can estimate the value a person puts on their time by evaluating how much time it would take to optimize their decision, the estimated value of the money that could be saved by spending more time to optimize the transaction, and the point at which a person no longer feels it is worth their efforts. This is, of course, subjective, as the individual will place different values on their time depending on what else they are doing: if they are very busy, then they will place greater value on their time and will accept greater costs associated with satisficing.

GAMBLER'S FALLACY

When you apply the laws of probability incorrectly, odds are you have committed the 'gambler's fallacy'. Consider a roulette wheel: on each spin, you have a 50 per cent probability that the ball will land on red, and a 50 per cent chance it will land on black. No matter how many times it lands on red in a row, the next spin still has only a 50 per cent chance of landing on black. While it's true that the law of large numbers says that, given enough spins of the wheel, half the spins will be black and half red, this is a passive law—one that can only be observed—and does not actively cause the probability of each spin to change. Despite this, investors all too often make the critical mistake of assuming that the next spin after a run of reds is likely to be black.

All too often it's common for investors to say things like, 'I will just hold the investment until the price is back at the level at which I bought it' or, 'If I hold it long enough, the price will go back up,' as if there's some reason that it would not continue to drop in price. This also tends to be common with certain types of large purchases, wherein a person buys what's known as a 'money pit'. The current meaning of the term is attributed to an extremely deep, manmade pit on Canada's Oak Island, which many treasure hunters have spent millions attempting to excavate, without any success. In the same way, it's not uncommon for people to purchase a house or a car and spend more on repairs than it was originally worth, telling themselves that it will be fine after just one more fix. Unfortunately, even learning basic probability theory will only work if there are known probabilities, such as at the roulette table—with a money pit the probabilities aren't so clear. The best thing that can be done is to evaluate objectively the current value and costs of ownership, and to calculate the outcome that is most likely given the best information available.

DISPOSITION EFFECT

Closely related to the gambler's fallacy—and prone to exacerbating its effects—the disposition effect is where people are less willing to recognize their losses and more willing to accept their gains. This can cause them to continue taking on losses in the belief that an investment will regain its value, yet when an investment does increase in value, to sell it for fear that they may miss the peak price. There's an old cliché among investors that says you should buy low and sell high, meaning buy an investment when it's cheap and sell it when it's expensive, which is deceptive in its simplicity. Calculating the value and market price movement of an investment is a very difficult thing to do well, and impossible to do perfectly, except by luck. To determine when an investment is at its highest or lowest point is not something anyone can say with 100 per cent certainty. Seasoned investors will calculate upper and lower limits on price movements, as well as what they think the intrinsic value of the investment is, and then pre-set orders to execute when the investment reaches specific trigger prices, which can be helpful in mitigating the influence of the disposition effect. It can also be helpful to watch trends—if an investment continues to lose more value than you anticipated, sell it and rebuy it when you think it has started to rebound. When an investment is increasing in value rapidly, you may consider buying it, but get ready to sell it at a moment's notice in case it starts to stagnate. Online trading platforms have made this a cheap and easy process.

MISPERCEIVED RISK

Perception is a subjective thing, prone to error, and people may interpret the same event in very different ways depending on their perception. In hearing news about one of your investments, you may give too much or too little importance to that news, perhaps misinterpreting the probability of the news causing an impact on your portfolio. As discussed in chapter 7, it's common for people to confuse the relationship between risk and returns, causing them to incur fruitless risk. Many people also tend to underestimate the amount of risk involved through the illusion of control. Sometimes people believe they have greater control over their investment portfolios than they truly exert, as they refuse to acknowledge that the performance of the investments in their portfolio can be very volatile and can cause unexpected losses. This illusion tends to build during economic booms, and particularly during economic bubbles, while recessions shatter that and leave investors disillusioned.

PROSPECT THEORY

People have a tendency to think in extremes. We focus on the limits of what is possible and live for the improbable. When people gamble, it's always with the thought of winning big; when we buy insurance, it's always to mitigate the risk of rare events; and when we invest, it's more thrilling to chant the mantra 'no risk, no reward'. In other aspects of life, people shape the way they live based on the prospect of unlikely risks or rewards. Pascal's Wager perfectly illustrates this point: it proposes that the consequences of being wrong while not believing in the Christian God are much greater than being wrong while believing in Him, ergo being faithful is the logical choice. Pascal's Wager takes advantage of people's tendency to focus on the extreme consequences, no matter how unlikely. This behaviour has a direct impact on our finances, in that since risk is a type of cost (see chapter 7), people will overpay to manage it. Statistically, the insurance industry represents a collective overpayment of risk management, since insurance companies earn money by charging more in premiums than they pay in awards. People tend to underestimate or ignore the risks inherent in specific investments in the pursuit of high returns, taking greater losses as a result, since risk does not inherently come with greater returns (see p. 102). People would not gamble at all if not for the immensely unlikely promise of instant wealth.

Prospect theory encompasses behaviours that are caused by emotional stimulation. Calculating the probability of what is most likely to occur is boring for most people, while learning what the extreme benefits or losses could be creates a strong emotional response. These behaviours can be disrupted, however, by ignoring your initial response. Regardless of how you feel about the financial choice you face, take the time to do some quick calculations to determine the most probable outcome and, if you want to get a little fancy, what range of values are likely to be encountered within a 95 per cent or 99 per cent probability. (For those familiar with basic statistics, confidence intervals are crucial in doing this.)

EMOTIONAL INFLUENCE

Emotions provide a critical function in daily life, but we need to be careful to ensure that they don't cause us to act in a manner inconsistent with our environment. People often underestimate how much influence our emotions have on our financial decisions. It seems odd to many that an irrational and passionate emotional response can influence, or even be created by, rational, quantitative activity such as banking or investing. Watching the stock markets, though, has shown conclusively that generally happy people take greater financial risk, while pessimists tend to estimate more accurately the intrinsic value of an investment. Day to day, if people read an exciting story in the news that morning (even news completely unrelated to investing), stock prices tend to increase more, as people feel confident and are willing to take greater risk, or see greater potential in investments. If there are reports of bad news, then stocks tend to decline or grow more slowly, as investors tolerate significantly less risk in their portfolios.

Finance itself can become a self-perpetuating emotional rollercoaster—there is psychological reward associated with spending or investing, as well as the psychological punishment associated with losing money. When you spend money, it releases dopamine and other chemicals in the brain called neurotransmitters, giving you a feeling of happiness, excitement and euphoria, motivating you to spend more. When you manage your own money or manage the money of others, the act of investing can be extremely thrilling. It is similar to gambling in that people put their money at risk for huge potential gains; they get a huge emotional reward when it happens and a huge emotional punishment when they lose, but either way they feel motivated to continue investing with larger amounts and taking greater risks.

Consider for a moment you are going grocery shopping. When you go to the shop while hungry, everything looks delicious, and you will tend to buy all sorts of things you don't need and probably shouldn't be eating. Our shopping is much more rational when we go after having eaten, allowing us to focus more on what we will need. This difference is caused by nothing more than a shift in emotional response, triggered by variations in hunger; when we are hungry, all the food we see appears to have much more utility than it really does, causing us to use our money in a manner that is less than optimal. The insidious part of emotional influence on our financial decisions is that we are generally not aware it's happening. We like to think that our decisions are rational—based on logical evaluation of the costs and benefits associated with the decision—so we aren't prone to questioning whether our choices are sound. There is no trick to bypass this behaviour, but it is possible to recognize when we are being emotional and to try to rely on decisions or calculations we have performed in a calm, premeditated manner. Determine in advance what it is that you plan to accomplish with your investments, and take the extra time to revisit the decision more than once, in the hope that assessing your options under varied emotional states will give greater insight into not only the decision, but also your own tendencies.

MENTAL ACCOUNTING

Many people have a 'rainy day fund': money set aside in case of some large, unexpected cost, a period of unemployment or another significant, short-term financial problem. A huge number of people have retirement accounts that are completely separate from their bank accounts or even other brokerage accounts. Some married couples keep separate bank accounts. Some people go as far as to open bank accounts dedicated to specific goals, like saving for university, buying an engagement ring, taking a mortgage, and so forth. Others keep money hidden at home. Few of these people can clearly articulate exactly why they have these separate accounts; if pressed, they might say 'that's what you're supposed to do', or they might reference an unspecified risk. This activity of having separate accounts simply for the sake of having separate accounts, is called 'mental accounting'.

As we discussed in chapter 9, retirement accounts have a very valid purpose. Some banks offer benefits if you open an account before taking a loan. If you have a lot of money, then opening several accounts can be a matter of ensuring your deposits are federally insured. The point is, if you have multiple accounts, make sure there is actually a valid reason for doing so, and that you will benefit more than if you had kept everything in a single account.

ANCHORING

Anchoring is the formal term for a financial 'rule of thumb'. This includes reference points that are generally accepted among sociocultural groups but which are completely arbitrary. A common anchor is that you should buy an engagement ring worth two months of your net salary. It's nonsense. Another common anchor is that when you buy a house, your mortgage payments should be between 25–35 per cent of your monthly gross income, depending on to whom you are talking. The size of house you need has nothing to do with your income, and the less money you make, the more of your total income you are going to spend on it. The poor and working classes spend 99–100 per cent of everything they make on basic subsistence, and housing generally composes between 50–75 per cent of that. If they have kids, then finding a house with payments which are 25 per cent of their monthly income becomes preposterous. One's housing needs increase much more slowly than one's income, so the more money you make, the smaller the percentage of your monthly income spent on housing will be.

The bottom line is that there's no one-size-fits-all answer to any financial decision. These anchors are total nonsense, developed by people trying to pass themselves off as experts. Determine what your needs are and make decisions based on that, not based on the needs of someone who thinks everyone should do as they do.

FRAMING

If I told you the stock of ABC Company had lost 50 per cent of its value in a sudden bout of volatility, you would likely find that stock somewhat terrifying. On the other hand, if I told you that the stock of ABC Company had lost 50 per cent of its value as a result of a market that overreacted to a one-time loss resulting from a natural disaster, then you may consider buying up as much as you can. Both statements say essentially the same thing but were framed in different ways. Studies have shown that the way information is presented is actually more important than the information itself in shaping how people respond. Given the exact same information and the exact same options, but each time worded differently, people will make the choices that appear to maximize benefits rather than cause harm, even if the option that appears to maximize benefits actually causes more harm. An example gives respondents the opportunity to either save 80 per cent of people or kill 10,000; people generally choose to save the 80 per cent, even if that actually results in more people dying.

Our psychological frame is composed of everything we have learned up until that point. Our knowledge, culture, emotional responses, learned behaviours and genetics have shaped how we interpret the world around us and, as a result, shape how we make and respond to decisions. As a result, the way information is presented will alter the way we have learned to respond to that information by causing us to pull from different experiences, alter our emotional response, and so forth. This is commonly used by physicians when presenting bad news: they will offer the news first in technical jargon to ease the patient into it, and then use the common words they will understand but with emotional triggers. This also means that the financial decisions we make are prone not only to subjective error, but also to direct manipulation. The only piece of investing advice I give to prospective investors is not to trust anyone giving them investing advice, particularly people on the news. Even assuming they know what they are talking about and are correct in their statements, you don't know what their own investing strategy is. In the US, it's common to see advertisements for companies that will buy gold and jewellery for cash when the price of gold is low, and then more advertisements telling you that gold is the best investment on earth when the price is high again. Carefully derive the core facts from the information to which you are exposed and throw away all the opinions, editorials and recommendations. After all, investors don't become successful by giving away their secrets.

NEPOTISM

It exists in every culture as an engrained social mechanism: in China it's known as *guanxi*; in Russia they call it *blat*; Arabic-speaking countries refer to it as *wasta*; while some circles in Western countries would recognize it as 'the good old boys' network'; but it all refers to the same thing—nepotism. In the financial context, nepotism occurs when you fail to optimize a financial decision by giving precedence to someone with whom you have a social connection. Most commonly it refers to the practice of hiring employees or giving business to people who are friends or relatives, rather than the most qualified person—this can include financial advisors and brokers, or whom you purchase goods or services from. Regardless of the circumstances, nepotism takes place when a person places greater value on maintaining a social relationship than on the differential in qualifications between their friend and the best candidate. The result is that you get less value for your money or you pay more money.

It's natural for people to value their relationships with other people. Not only are we social animals that have evolved to compete collectively for resources against other species, but the entire global economy is based on our ability to specialize in a narrow range of skills, and then trade with people who specialized in other areas, creating what's known as 'gains from trade'. We also tend to gravitate naturally towards people whose company we enjoy, whom we feel we can trust or who may be able to provide reciprocation at a later date. However, while all these things may provide some benefit, they do cause us to make decisions which, in that instance, are less than optimal.

OBSERVATION EFFECT

People change their behaviour when they know they are being observed in a phenomenon known as the 'observation effect'. For example, it is common for people to lie on surveys when the truth may be something that others would find distasteful. It is for this reason that US governmental research on the number of people who use drugs and their frequency of use tends to understate the reality horribly (it is estimated by between 40–70 per cent). Studies on social accountability demonstrate that when people are paired off, and one is given a stack of money, of which they are free to give their partner as much or little as they like, they only share the money when the two partners can see each other, and keep it when they cannot. The observation effect makes research in economics, psychology and other behavioural fields tricky. In the real world, it poses a concern for budgeting and evaluating your spending behaviour, because when you carefully track your spending for a period of time, the extra attention will fundamentally alter your behaviour, so that the period being studied does not resemble your typical spending behaviour. In other words, when you pay closer attention, you will tend to have better spending habits than when you satisfice and allow impulse to have a greater influence.

Depending on the circumstances, this can actually work to your advantage. Sure, there is the issue of complicating your own, personal research into your spending habits, but thanks to debit cards and electronic banking, you can track your normal spending behaviour in hindsight by looking at your debit account history. The observation effect can actually help you develop positive spending habits; it's all a matter of creating the illusion of direct accountability. Train yourself to imagine that someone you know is able to see your purchases, particularly someone who also relies on your financial decisions. What would they have you do in that situation? This may sound a bit paranoid, perhaps, but the goal is to use this as a temporary measure until your positive spending habits become second nature.

ENDOWMENT EFFECT

My stuff is better than your stuff. Even if we have the exact same stuff, mine is still more valuable. That's the basic premise of a phenomenon known as the 'endowment effect': people place a higher value on possessions that they own than on the exact same possessions owned by someone else. This subjective, erroneous perception of value may sound like a problem exclusive to secondhand stores and yard sales, but it becomes a more serious concern when it influences your investment decisions. The differential in perception of value can cause a person to forego purchasing an undervalued investment, or to refuse to sell an overvalued one. The trick to short-circuiting this tendency is to use an objective evaluation and consistently apply it to all investments, regardless of ownership.

BIASES

When people want to believe something, they subconsciously ensure that all the information they receive is processed as confirming their beliefs. This is known as 'confirmation bias'. Once a person has formed an idea about the way things are, they often feel threatened by information that contradicts that idea. This doesn't happen right away—a person that receives contradicting information too soon after being exposed to the original idea will become confused, but if some time has passed and the person has a chance to integrate the idea into their overall worldview, then challenging that idea causes a fear response that can be very strong. As a result, people will disregard or deny any contradictory information and will intentionally seek information that confirms their beliefs, regardless of how unreliable the source.

Ideas that contradict one's beliefs aren't the only form of information that can scare people. In fact, any sort of change can be quite terrifying. People are creatures of habit who actively seek consistent, stable patterns, and when faced with the prospect of change they often become averse or hostile. Even when given the opportunity to change something that they don't like, people will frequently simply opt to suffer. This is known as a 'status quo bias', wherein people avoid change at all cost. So, for example, if a better financial option is available than the one you currently have, you may feel resistant to take it up simply to avoid change.

A 'home bias' is the tendency to prefer domestic investments to international ones based on an irrational sense of safety that has nothing to do with the domestic investments themselves and more to do with a fear of traits in international investments that they don't understand. Maybe the investment requires them to interact with people who adhere to unfamiliar cultural traits or who speak a language they don't know, or the investment functions within a country they have never been to. This aversion response can be seen across society: it is common to see migrants of a similar background live in the same geographic area, such as 'Chinatowns', just as it's common for expat workers to gravitate towards each other for social interaction, even if their original intent was to integrate with the local people, simply because it requires less effort. In the same way, it's common for people to prefer investments and other financial products associated with cultures and people with which they are most familiar, though they may cite 'safety' as the reason why.

Self-serving bias is an all too common way of protecting one's own self-esteem. Simply, a self-serving bias is one in which a person gives himself credit for his successes but blames outside factors, such as other people, for his failures. It can be difficult to accept that you are flawed (and we are all flawed in many ways), but rather than accept this and learn from it, people have a tendency to point their finger at everything around them to find a scapegoat upon which they can place blame for mistakes or failures. By contrast, when something good happens, people tend to try to take credit for it, saying that they *earned* it, or *deserve* it, as a direct result of their actions, rather than giving credit to the external factors that facilitated their success. This is an extremely competitive mind-set, which helps people to justify their role within a socioeconomic context and within a competitive pursuit of scarce resources, including intangible resources like job promotions or esteem.

All these biases are unique in the manner in which they erroneously process information but alike in their use of selective acceptance of information. These selective criteria for the acceptance or rejection of data to which a person is exposed shape their beliefs and, as a result, the decisions they make. As finances are very sensitive to our behavioural idiosyncrasies, each of these biases has a distinct and identifiable impact on the way people manage their money. We must remain aware of them in order to mitigate the costs we incur as a result.

PSYCHOLOGICAL ILLNESS

The anomalies discussed in this chapter are ones that are present in almost all people—they are a part of human psychology. However, there are times when abnormal psychology has a predictable and measurable impact on one's finances too. Psychological illness causes a negative impact on an individual's life in a number of ways, including, commonly, financial hardship. For example, addiction often leads a person to lose their possessions and even their source of income as they spend all their money on their compulsion, and eventually the negative effects begin to interfere with their work and investments. People who are suicidal will quite frequently attempt to give away all their money and possessions to the people they love or to charity, as a final act of settling one's estate. People who are manic or bipolar tend to go through periods of extreme purchasing, buying extravagant gifts for themselves and others—things that they simply can't afford. People with certain types of schizophrenia will sometimes spend their money erratically. Individuals with autism spectrum disorder (ASD) can be very meticulous with their finances if offered an environment in which they can learn how, but have severe difficulty maintaining a consistent source of income, as over 80 per cent of people with ASD sustain long-term unemployment.

Psychological illnesses are very often accompanied by financial hardships, which is easy to lump into a single generalization. By looking closer at the specific financial behaviours being exhibited, however, it becomes clear that different types of financial behaviours are trademarks of specific mental conditions, not only allowing one to properly respond to the symptoms of these conditions and improve their financial management, but even providing the potential to contribute to diagnostic evaluations. Regardless of whether a particular behaviour is the result of a sickness, or present in all people after millennia of evolution as a species, the behaviours we exhibit influence our financial decisions, preventing us from realizing our true wealth potential. It is only by understanding what these behaviours are that we can recognize them and develop strategies to cope with them to improve our financial management.

CONCLUSION

All these elements of personal finance fit together like puzzle pieces to provide a comprehensive set of tools intended to assist you in managing your finances. Data from the income statement (chapter 2) explains changes in the total value of the balance sheet (chapter 6), while the personal statement of cash flows (chapter 8) provides additional details about the sources of income and costs. Opportunities for your debt (chapter 5), investments (chapter 6), costs (chapter 4) and income (chapter 8) dictate your budget, while the budget itself (chapter 2) provides data for all three major financial statements. The budget is used to track changes, while major financial statements are used to track macro trends in your financial health, wealth management and retirement planning (chapter 9). While each element of a comprehensive financial management system can provide vital information, it is only one piece of the overall puzzle, and cannot provide all the information you need to make important financial decisions. In the same way, this book is only one resource available to you as you improve your financial management. This is an introductory book that provides the basics of personal financial management. Every chapter would warrant its own book if we were to delve fully into a comprehensive explanation of each.

Even then, there are issues outside of finance itself that influence your finances, such as economic and sociopolitical factors, on which I have written other books, if you are interested in continuing to learn more about optimizing your wealth. Books you may want to explore include *101 Things Everyone Needs to Know about the Global*

Economy (Adams Media); *Corporate Finance for Dummies* (John Wiley & Sons); and the trilogy *Economics and Modern Warfare, Psychology and Modern Warfare*, and *Analytics and Modern Warfare* (Palgrave Macmillan).

Still, having all the tools in the world will not create miracles. You actually need to use them and get lots of practice. The impact that this book will have on your finances will be entirely dependent on whether you have the inclination to implement the tools and learn the techniques to use them. The world in which we live is dynamic, so it's not enough to put your finances on 'autopilot'—establishing a system that is optimal at the moment it was created and then ignoring it. Your finances are always changing, and the world in which your financial concerns exist changes even more quickly; so due diligence is not only helpful—it's critical. Establish a schedule for financial management—check elements regularly, whether daily, weekly, monthly, quarterly or yearly. You can't accomplish your financial goals simply by learning about your money—you must manage your money.

GLOSSARY

A

Annuity: A financial product similar to insurance, but which functions as an income-generating investment rather than a risk management tool.

Ask price: The price at which investors are willing to sell a bond.

Asset-backed securities (ABS): Ownership of specific investments or operations, rather than ownership in a company.

B

Bankruptcy: A legally obligated restructuring or forgiveness of debt obligations.

Bearer bond: Outdated form of bond, of which the person currently in possession of the bond is recognized as its owner. Now largely replaced by *Registered bonds*.

Bid price: The price at which investors are willing to buy a bond.

Bond: An investment in the debt of an organization.

Budget: A periodic estimation of resource volume and distribution.

Buying on margin: Buying stock using borrowed money. You must eventually repay that money with interest, so this is only effective if your stock earnings are higher than your interest rate.

C

Callable bonds: A special type of bond that gives the issuer the option to recall their bonds by paying the current value plus a penalty to the issuer, should interest rates drop enough that the penalties are less than the amount saved by issuing bonds at the lower interest rates.

Cap: An indicator of the size of a company's market capitalization (the collective value of their stocks), from 'large' caps (>$10 billion) to 'nano' caps (<$50 million).

Chips: Stocks issued by particular sectors—e.g., 'blue chip' are issued by large, global corporations, 'green chip' are issued by companies that work in environmental sustainability industries, and 'red chip' are issued by Chinese companies in a market outside China.

Common stock: A stock that allows you to vote on the board of directors and on certain corporate decisions, and gives you rights to corporate financial information and any profits not used as retained earnings or to pay the dividends of preferred stockholders, in a split equal to the number of shares outstanding (the total number of shares of stock which are owned).

Constructive debt: Debt in which the money is used to generate income or wealth at a higher rate than the interest it accrues.

Convertible bonds: A special type of corporate bond (issued by a corporation) that gives you the option to exchange the bond for a given number of shares of stock.

Corporate bonds: Bonds issued by corporations—they vary widely in rate and risk.

Coupon bonds: Whereas typical bonds pay their total value upon maturity, coupon bonds make several payments ('coupons') over the course of their life, maturity simply being the final payment.

Credit quality: The amount of risk that an issuer has of defaulting, as assessed by underwriters.

D

Debt reorganization: A change in the value and costs of several loans through planned repayment strategies.

Deferment: A temporary halt of loan repayment obligations.

Derivatives: Contracts for the exchange of investments that are bought and sold prior to the actual exchange.

Destructive debt: Debt that has higher interest rate costs than the amount of income or wealth generated through the use of borrowed funds.

Discount/Rate: Bonds are sold at a price lower than the face value in an amount equivalent to the amount of interest the bond will earn upon maturity; they are said to be sold at a 'discount' of their *Face value*.

Discretionary income: The amount of remaining income after all legal and subsistence expenses are paid.

Diversification: The act of investing in several different investments to reduce the potential value of loss if a single investment fails.

Double-entry accounting: A system of financial record keeping that ties changes in the value of one account to an opposite change in value to another account.

E

Escrow: Custody through a third party until a specified condition has been met.

Estimated value: The monetary value that is predicted based on trends and/or calculations.

Expected shortfall (ES): An estimation of the maximum amount of financial losses that could potentially be experienced, though unlikely.

F

Face value/Par value: The amount of money that will be given to the bond holder on maturity of the bond.

Fiat currency: Any currency which derives its value from the value of the resource exchanges it represents.

Fixed-rate loan: A loan that charges a constant rate of interest.

Forward: A customizable contract that guarantees the terms of exchange at a future date.

Future: A standardized contract that guarantees the terms of exchange at a future date, which can be traded like equities.

Future value: The monetary value of an investment or account at any future time.

G

Government bonds: Bonds issued by governments can range widely in time to maturity, but short-term government debt lasting 30 days or fewer is considered a risk-free rate, since government debt tends to be safer than other types. Some have tax exemptions, depending on the country.

H

Home equity lines of credit (HELOC): A line of credit that uses home equity as collateral.

Horizontal analysis: An assessment that calculates financial changes over time.

Hybrid-rate loan: A loan that has elements of both a fixed-rate and variable-rate loan.

I

Inflation: A reduction in the purchasing power of a currency.

Investment: Any expenditure made with the expectation of increased value over time.

Issuer: The organization which initially sells the bond, and who will repay its value.

J

Junk bonds: Bonds issued by issuers with a very high risk of default. The higher risk means they have to offer higher interest rates to attract investors.

L

Lagging indicators: Measurements of past events that allow you to assess financial behaviour over a period of time.

Lien: Legal right to ownership of property by a lender in the case of default.

Limit order: An order to buy a stock when its price rises to a given price at which the investor feels that the stock will continue to maintain stable growth, or to sell it at that high price if the investor believes the price will drop again after reaching a peak.

Lines of credit: A type of loan in which money can be continuously borrowed and repaid at the discretion of the borrower.

Long (buying or selling): A standard transaction, wherein any changes in value are directly and instantly yours to incur. Buy long when you think the price will go up; sell long when you think the price will go down.

M

Marginal propensity to consume (MPC): The proportion of total income that is spent.

Marginal propensity to save (MPS): The proportion of total income that is saved.

Market orders: Orders that occur at current market price.

Market risk: Risk of financial loss resulting from overall economic decline.

Maturity: The date at which a bond will be repaid by the issuer.

Money: Any store of resource value owed to the owner.

Mortgage-backed security (MBS): The most common type of asset-backed security, in which a bank raises money by selling shares of MBS to mortgage borrowers to buy homes, who then repay their principal, the interest or both to the investor.

N

Net present value (NPV): The sum of present values on an investment that generates multiple cash flows.

O

Observed value: The monetary value that is actually experienced.

Option: A contract that gives the purchaser the right, and the seller the obligation, to participate in an exchange at established terms should the purchaser choose to exercise their right.

P

Pegged orders: Orders that do not execute until some trigger other than the stock's price is observed, such as a change in value of a stock index or in some economic metric like employment.

Penny stocks: Extremely cheap stocks, with a price of less than $0.01, which must often be bought and sold in blocks. They belong to very small firms in industries conducting uncertain research or creating experimental products, or in new industries. They sometimes can indicate fraudulent operations.

Personal income statement: A report of a person's or household's income, expenditures and financial gains and losses.

Preferred stock: A lot like common stock, except that it doesn't give you voting rights, but it does give you guaranteed dividends.

Present value: The value that an investment with known future value has at the present time.

Price: The price for which bonds are selling.

Price change: The amount of change in a bond's price over the previous period.

Purchase: Any expenditure made with the expectation of lost value over time.

Purchasing power: The ability of a fiat currency to be exchanged for goods and services.

Puttable bonds: A special type of bond that gives the investor the option to force the issuer to repay the value of the bond minus a penalty.

R

Registered bond: A modern form of bond, given a serial number which 'registers' the bond to its owner. Replaces *Bearer bonds*.

Resale value: The price at which an item can be resold after a period of ownership.

Retirement accounts: Accounts that are given preferential tax status when specific criteria towards retirement are met.

Reverse mortgage: A type of home equity loan in which the lender takes the house after the borrower dies in lieu of loan repayment.

Riders: Contractual additions to an annuity that can be purchased for an additional fee.

Risk: The probability and value of financial loss.

S

Scrap value: The price at which an item can be sold for scrap or parts after its useful life has been consumed.

Short (selling): Borrowing a stock and selling it to someone else with a promise to repurchase it at a later date; done when you think a stock will go down in price.

Simple interest: The accrual of interest income or payments at a constant rate.

Specific risk: Risk that is associated with an individual investment.

Spread: The difference between the *Ask* and *Bid* prices. The sale of bonds only occurs when an investor is willing to increase their bid or decrease their ask to a value attractive to other investors.

Stop order: An order to sell a stock when its price drops below a given price to limit potential losses, or to buy a stock when it reaches that low price if the investor believes the price will go back up.

T

Time-contingent orders: Orders that are put on a time delay or cancelled after a given amount of time.

Transferability: A characteristic (of a credit) of being able to readily transfer or exchange ownership.

V

Value at risk (VaR): An estimation of the maximum amount of financial losses likely to be experienced.

Variable-rate loan: A loan that charges a rate of interest which is subject to change.

Vertical analysis: An assessment that calculates the composition of financial allocations.

Volume: The number of bonds bought or sold during a given period.

W

Warranty: A contractual guarantee by a manufacturer or seller to incur some or all of the financial risk associated with the chance of faulty or damaged products.

Y

Yield: The rate of returns a person will experience by purchasing a bond at a particular price in a given year.

Yield change: The amount of change in a bond's yield over the previous period.

Yield to maturity (YTM): The rate of returns a person will experience if the bond and all coupons are held until the maturity date.

TEMPLATES

PERSONAL INCOME STATEMENT

Net Sales Source 1	$
Net Sales Source 2	$
Total Net Income	$

COGS Source 1	$
COGS Source 2	$
COGS Source 3	$
Total COGS	$

Gross Margin	$
Operational Expense 1	$
Operational Expense 2	$
Operational Expense 3	$
Total Operational Expenses	$

One-Time Earnings/Losses	$
EBIT	$
Tax and Interest Payments	$
Net Income	$

BUDGET

	Estimated value ($)	Percentage of total	Cumulative percentage	Observed value ($)	Difference (%)
Available assets			100%		
Taxes					
Disposable income			–		
Item 1					
Item 2					
Discretionary income			–		
Retirement					
Investments					
Savings					
Luxuries					

PERSONAL BALANCE SHEET

$X	$X
Assets	**Debt**
Item 1	Item 1
Item 2	Item 2
Item 3	**Equity**
Item 4	Item 1
Item 5	Item 2

PERSONAL STATEMENT OF CASH FLOWS

Operating activities

Cash inflows

Item 1 $

Item 2 $

Cash outflows

Item 1 $

Item 2 $

Investing activities

Cash inflows

Item 1 $

Item 2 $

Cash outflows

Item 1 $

Item 2 $

Financing activities

Cash inflows

Item 1 $

Item 2 $

Cash outflows

Item 1 $

Item 2 $

NOTES

You can use the following pages to make your own notes on any of the exercises in the book.